# STICK TO BASICS

You are enough the way you are

YATIKA TYAGI

**InkSpire Publishers**
Proud Imprint of Noverse Foundation

Dwarikapuri, Muzzaffarnagar, Uttar Pradesh - 251001

Website: www.inkspirepublishers.com

Email id: publishersinkspire@gmail.com

Instagram: inkspirepublishers


Author – Yatika Tyagi
Book Title: STICK TO THE BASICS
ISBN: 978-81-971023-5-6
Price: ₹399


Processed and printed in India.

# Acknowledgements

My heart is filled with gratitude towards each and every person in my life who guided me and motivated me to write this book. It's not one day job but took years of experience to come up with something like this. This book is enriched with a lot of learning which I have learnt and implemented myself through the course of my life. It is a true journey within self.

**"तस्मै श्री गुरवे नमः"**

This book is dedicated to my Guru who is an epitome of unconditional love and support. I have learnt – How to live meaningful Life. His teachings inspired me to write this book as a small contribution from my side which may help many to improve their life as well.

**"माता गुरुतरा भूमेः खात् पितोच्चतरस्तथा"**

This Sanskrit shloka glorifies parents' significance in life and here it goes- The mother's glory excels the earth's weight and the father honour surpasses the sky. I could not have achieved anything without their selfless love, support, and blessings. I cannot express how much I owe to them. Thank you for everything you have done for me. Both my parents are my strength and inspiration.

I express endless gratitude towards my husband and two adorable kids; for being so loving and supportive. A huge Thanks to my extended family, friends and well-wishers.

I am grateful to Aakarsh and his team at InkSpire Publishers for their support in publishing this book.

And finally, a massive thank you to all the readers who have chosen to read my first book. I am sure it will help you find your true worth and always remember that "YOU ARE ENOUGH".

## Author's Message- How to read the Book

I have written this book with a purpose. Here my Goal is to help the reader to look at their life from another perspective. Everyone has a unique journey and has their struggles in life. Some succumb to their circumstances and some dare to beat all odds. How the perception of looking at life matters. And this is the only thing which helps to overcome any situation in life. It's just a matter of mindset.

So, before you start reading this book, make sure you are ready to explore yourself. There are chapters which will make you understand that how and where you were messing up with your life- there you need to be true to yourself. No one is watching you or pushing you to be someone else, therefore it's you who has to design your life. If you want to live a happy and contented life; be ready to transform your inner self.

You may find that some of the concepts are repeated and going the same way as explained in previous chapters. This is just a reminder that life is simple and works on a few basic principles. You just need to stick to basics and that is to be happy in your skin.

I am sure this book will change your life too. I wish all the best for your new journey to become alive.

# Contents

# Introduction

Welcome, dear reader, and prepare to embark on a journey of self-discovery, empowerment, and enlightenment. The world, in all its vast complexity and challenging circumstances, can often make us feel insignificant, insufficient, or inadequate. This book is here to tell you otherwise. It is here to tell you that you are enough.

Many of us spend our lives in a constant state of comparison, always measuring ourselves against others and falling short in our own eyes. We are plagued by self-doubt, insecurities, and the feeling of never being enough. But what if we told you that you are enough, just as you are, right at this moment? What if we told you that you, with your unique abilities, talents, and experiences, can enlighten this world?

This book is not just a testament to your significance, but a call to action. It is a call to stop questioning your worth and start realizing your potential. It is a call to embrace your flaws, recognize your strengths, and understand that your journey is unique and valuable. It is a call to stop shrinking yourself to fit into boxes designed by society and start expanding to fill the universe with your incredible light.

This book is a guide to finding your inner power and using it to contribute to the world in ways you never thought possible. It is a guide to understanding that you are not just a tiny speck in the universe, but a vital part of it. It is a guide to realizing that you are not incomplete or inadequate, but whole and enough, just as you are.

As you turn the pages, you will find stories, experiences, and lessons that will inspire, motivate, and empower you. You will learn that you are more than your mistakes, more than your fears, and more than the labels others have placed on you. You will learn that you are a beacon of light in this world and that you have the power to enlighten it with your existence.

So, dear reader, dive into this journey of self-discovery and enlightenment. Embrace the truth that you are enough and that you have the power to make a difference. Remember, the world needs your light. You are enough, and you can enlighten this world.

# Chapter 1: Embracing Individuality

## Understanding Your Uniqueness

Every person is a universe unto themselves, a complex and unique blend of experiences, dreams, and traits. But in a world that often seems to favor conformity and sameness, it can be challenging to recognize and embrace our uniqueness. Yet, it is this very uniqueness that makes us enough, exactly as we are.

In every moment of every day, you are a unique expression of life. You are the only person in the world who has lived your life, experienced what you have, and sees the world through your eyes. This is a profound realization, one that can change the way you perceive yourself and your value. Your uniqueness is not a flaw or a quirk to be hidden away. It is a strength, an asset, a testament to the diversity and beauty of human existence.

Consider your fingerprints. They are uniquely yours, a physical representation of your individuality. Just as no two fingerprints are the same, no two people share the same combination of experiences, perspectives, and talents. This means that you can contribute something to the world that nobody else can, simply by being you.

It is your unique blend of strengths and weaknesses, victories and struggles, dreams and fears that make you who you are. You are not a clone, a replica, or a second-rate version of someone else. You are an original, and in that originality, you will find your greatest strength.

Embracing your uniqueness also means accepting your imperfections. In a society that often rewards perfection and success, it's easy to feel that our flaws and failures diminish our worth. But the truth is, our imperfections are part of what makes us unique. They are part of our story, our journey, our humanity.

Your uniqueness is not just about what you do or what you have achieved. It's also about who you are at your core. It's about your values, your passions, your beliefs. It's about the way you laugh, the things that make you cry, the causes that stir your heart.

Understanding your uniqueness is not a one-time event. It's a journey, a process of self-discovery that unfolds over a lifetime. It involves asking questions, seeking understanding, and continually growing and evolving. It involves being true to yourself, even when it's tempting to blend in or conform.

There is no one else in the world who can be you. This is your power. This is your magic. This is your gift to the world. So, embrace your uniqueness. Celebrate it. Share it. Because you, in all your unique glory, are more than enough.

In the end, understanding your uniqueness is about recognizing and honoring the incredible individual that you are. It's about seeing your value, your worth, your potential. It's about realizing that you are not just a drop in the ocean, but the entire ocean in a drop. You are not just a face in the crowd, but a unique and irreplaceable masterpiece. You are not just a voice in the choir, but a song that has never been sung before. And you, just as you are, are enough.

## The Power of Authenticity

In the journey of our existence, authenticity emerges as a potent force, a beacon that guides us towards our true selves. This is not a mere concept, but a fundamental truth that is often veiled by the masks we wear, the roles we play, and the expectations we strive to meet.

Our society often encourages conformity, subtly pressuring us to fit into pre-defined molds. We are taught to suppress our true selves in favor of a more 'acceptable' and 'likeable' persona. The fear of rejection and judgment can be overwhelming, leading us to hide our true selves. We may even go as far as to adopt traits, opinions, and habits that are not our own, just to blend in. This can lead to a life of pretense, a life that lacks authenticity.

However, when we truly embrace our authenticity, it becomes a powerful tool for self-discovery and personal growth. It allows us to break free from the shackles of societal expectations and live life on our terms. It enables us to express our true feelings, desires, and beliefs without the fear of being judged or criticized. It gives us the courage to stand up for what we believe in, even when it goes against the norm.

Authenticity also fosters self-acceptance. By acknowledging and embracing our strengths and weaknesses, our successes and failures, our joys and pains, we start to appreciate ourselves for who we truly are. We become comfortable in our own skin, and that in itself is a liberating experience. We realize that we are not defined by our past, our mistakes, or our shortcomings. We are defined by our ability to stay true to ourselves in a world that constantly tries to make us something else.

Moreover, authenticity helps us build genuine and meaningful relationships. When we are authentic, we attract people who appreciate us for our true selves, not for the image we project. These are the relationships that provide us with a safe space to express our thoughts and feelings without the fear of being judged or misunderstood. They provide us with the support and encouragement we need to grow and evolve.

In our pursuit of authenticity, we must remember that it's not about being perfect. It's about being real. It's about acknowledging our flaws and still choosing to love ourselves. It's about letting go of the need to be liked by everyone and focusing on being loved by the right people. It's about being brave enough to show our vulnerability and strong enough to admit our mistakes.

Authenticity, therefore, is not just about being true to others; it's about being true to ourselves. It's about honoring our values, following our passion, and living our truth. It's about finding the courage to be ourselves, despite the pressures to conform. It's about understanding that we are enough, just as we are.

So, let's embrace our authenticity. Let's shed the masks we wear and reveal our true selves. Let's celebrate our uniqueness and honor our individuality. Because in the end, the most beautiful and powerful thing we can be is ourselves. Because we are enough.

## Avoiding Comparison Traps

In our journey to self-acceptance and the realization that we are enough, one of the most common obstacles we encounter is the tendency to compare ourselves with others. This habit of comparison is deeply ingrained in our culture, our society, and our individual psyches. It is a trap that we often fall into, sometimes without even realizing it. In fact, every individual on this earth is taught to compare with others just to check where he stands. This brings low self-esteem or ego- believe me both are very dangerous for personal growth.

Comparison can be a useful tool in certain contexts. For instance, it can help us gauge our progress, identify areas of improvement, and set realistic goals. However, when used inappropriately, it can lead to feelings of inadequacy, anxiety, and self-doubt. It can make us feel as though we are constantly falling behind, not living up to expectations, or not good enough.

The comparison trap is particularly insidious because it is often based on skewed perceptions and unrealistic standards. We tend to compare our behind-the-scenes with other people's highlight reels. We see their successes, achievements, and perfect Instagram photos, and we feel inferior because we are acutely aware of our own struggles, failures, and imperfections.

Moreover, we tend to compare ourselves with the best in each category, setting ourselves up for failure. We compare our looks with those of models, our intelligence with that of geniuses, our success with that of billionaires. This is not a fair or realistic comparison. It is important to remember that everyone has their strengths and weaknesses, their successes and failures. No one is perfect, and no one has it all.

In order to avoid the comparison trap, we need to shift our focus from others to ourselves. Instead of comparing ourselves with others, we should compare ourselves with our past selves. We should strive to be better than we were yesterday, last week, last month, last year. This is a more constructive and empowering form of comparison. It encourages growth, progress, and self-improvement.

Another way to avoid the comparison trap is to practice gratitude. When we are grateful for what we have, we are less likely to covet what others have. We are less likely to feel inadequate or inferior. We are more likely to feel content, fulfilled, and enough.

It is also important to challenge the societal and cultural norms and standards that fuel the comparison trap. We need to question the idea that success equals wealth, that beauty equals thinness, that worth equals productivity. We need to redefine these concepts in a way that aligns with our values, our beliefs, our unique identities.

Finally, we need to cultivate self-compassion. We need to be kind to ourselves, to forgive ourselves for our mistakes and failures, to celebrate our successes and achievements, no matter how small. We need to love ourselves, not despite our imperfections, but because of them. Because they make us human, they make us real, they make us enough.

In conclusion, avoiding the comparison trap is not easy, but it is crucial in our journey to self-acceptance and self-love. It requires conscious effort, practice, and patience. But the reward is worth the struggle: a sense of inner peace, self-confidence, and self-worth that no external validation can ever provide. Because the truth is, we are enough, just as we are. And the sooner we realize this, the happier and more fulfilled we will be.

## Accepting Imperfections

As we journey through life, we often find ourselves striving for perfection, a pursuit that can bring both joy and frustration. The truth is, we are all wonderfully and beautifully flawed, and it is in these flaws that we find our unique strength and charm. The acceptance of imperfections, both in us and others, can indeed be a liberating experience.

Perfection is a myth, a mirage that continuously eludes us. It creates an illusion of a flawless existence, which is far from reality. In our pursuit of this illusion, we often forget to appreciate the beauty of our individuality, the charm of our idiosyncrasies, and the strength of our resilience. We tend to overlook the fact that each one of us is a work in progress, learning, growing, and evolving with every challenge and every victory.

Accepting our imperfections does not mean we stop striving for improvement or excellence. On the contrary, it means recognizing our limitations, acknowledging our failures, and understanding that it's okay to make mistakes. It's about embracing our unique journey of growth and self-improvement, where the goal is not to attain perfection, but to become the best version of ourselves.

The beauty of imperfection is that it allows us to be human, to be vulnerable. It gives us the freedom to make mistakes, to learn from them, and to grow. It teaches us to be compassionate towards ourselves and others, understanding that we all are fighting our unique battles and learning our individual lessons.

Accepting imperfections also opens the door to self-love and self-acceptance. It helps us to understand that we are enough, just as we are. We don't need to change ourselves to fit into someone else's idea of perfection. We don't need to compare ourselves with others and feel inadequate. We are unique, and it is this uniqueness that makes us special.

In our imperfections, we find our true selves. They are an integral part of our identity, shaping our character, and influencing our choices. They teach us humility, patience, and resilience. They help us to appreciate the journey of life, with all its twists and turns, highs and lows, joys and sorrows.

The acceptance of imperfections also fosters empathy and understanding. When we accept our flaws, we learn to accept the flaws of others. We learn to appreciate the diversity of human experience and understand that everyone is fighting their own battle, facing their own challenges, and dealing with their own insecurities.

In conclusion, accepting imperfections is not about settling for less or giving up on our dreams. It's about understanding and embracing our unique journey, with all its imperfections, and learning to love and accept ourselves for who we are. It's about celebrating our individuality, our uniqueness, and our resilience. It's about recognizing that we are enough, just as we are.

Remember, the pursuit of perfection may seem enticing, but it is the acceptance of imperfections that truly sets us free. So let's embrace our flaws, celebrate our uniqueness, and remember, we are enough, just as we are.

## Celebrating Your Identity

In the grand tapestry of life, each thread holds its unique color and texture, contributing to the beauty of the overall masterpiece. We, as individuals, are those threads, each with a distinctive identity that adds to the richness of humanity. Celebrating your identity is not merely acknowledging your unique traits but also rejoicing in the individual that you are.

In the journey of self-discovery, it's crucial to understand that your identity is multifaceted. It's a combination of your experiences, beliefs, values, and dreams. Each of these aspects is interwoven to create the person you are, and not one of them is insignificant. Just as a single thread can add depth to a tapestry, every part of your identity contributes to the richness of your being.

The celebration of your identity begins with self-acceptance. It's about embracing your strengths and weaknesses, triumphs and failures, hopes and fears. It's about acknowledging your imperfections and still seeing yourself as a beautiful, worthy individual. This acceptance is not a one-time act, but a continuous process. It involves forgiving yourself for past mistakes, being kind to yourself when you falter, and constantly encouraging yourself to grow and evolve.

However, self-acceptance doesn't mean you become complacent. Recognize that you are a work in progress and that growth is a fundamental part of your identity. Celebrating your identity means celebrating your ability to change and evolve. It's about seeing every experience, good or bad, as an opportunity to learn and grow. It's about understanding that you are not defined by your past, but by your ability to shape your future.

Furthermore, celebrating your identity is about honoring your uniqueness. It's about not conforming to societal norms or expectations and instead staying true to your authentic self. It's about not comparing yourself with others but appreciating the individual that you are. Remember, there is no one else like you in this world, and that is your superpower.

The celebration of your identity also extends to your relationships with others. It's about respecting others for their unique identities and not imposing your beliefs or values on them. It's about understanding that just as you have the right to celebrate your identity, so do others. This mutual respect and understanding foster a sense of unity in diversity, which is the essence of humanity.

In conclusion, celebrating your identity is an empowering journey of self-discovery, self-acceptance, and personal growth. It's about recognizing your worth and embracing your uniqueness. It's about understanding that you are enough, just as you are. So, revel in your identity, for it is the essence of your being, the core of your existence, and the source of your strength. Celebrate it, for it is what makes you, YOU.

# Chapter 2: Realizing Your Worth

## Reframing Negative Self-Talk

As we journey through life, we often become our own worst critics. The voices in our heads can be harsher than anyone else's, berating us for our mistakes, bemoaning our shortcomings, and belittling our achievements. This is what we refer to as negative self-talk, a destructive cycle that can feed our insecurities and diminish our self-esteem. But the power to alter this narrative lies within us, and the transformative art of reframing negative self-talk can help us reclaim our inner dialogue.

Reframing negative self-talk is not about denying or suppressing our feelings. Instead, it's about acknowledging our thoughts, understanding their origin, and then consciously choosing to interpret them in a more positive, empowering light. It's about cultivating a mindset of self-compassion, gentleness, and understanding, rather than one of self-criticism and judgment.

The first step in this process is awareness. To change our self-talk, we must first become aware of it. We must listen to that inner critic and recognize the patterns in its narrative. Is it constantly telling you that you're not good enough? That you're a failure? That you're unworthy of happiness or success? Once we have identified these patterns, we can begin to challenge them.

Challenging our negative self-talk involves questioning the validity of our inner critic's claims. Is it really true that we're not good enough? Or is this simply a belief that we've internalized over time due to past experiences or societal pressures? By questioning these beliefs, we can start to see them for what they truly are - distortions of reality, not absolute truths.

The next step is to replace these negative narratives with more positive, affirming ones. This might feel uncomfortable or even unnatural at first, but with practice, it can become second nature. Instead of telling ourselves that we're not good enough, we can remind ourselves that we are doing our best and that our worth is not defined by our mistakes or shortcomings. Instead of berating ourselves for our failures, we can celebrate our courage to try and our resilience to bounce back.

Reframing negative self-talk also involves cultivating a practice of self-compassion. This means treating ourselves with the same kindness, understanding, and forgiveness that we would extend to a dear friend. It means acknowledging that we are human, and like all humans, we are fallible. We make mistakes, we have flaws, and that's okay. It's part of being human.

Moreover, it's important to remember that reframing negative self-talk is not a one-time task, but an ongoing process. It requires patience, persistence, and practice. There will be times when we slip back into old patterns of thinking. But each time we catch ourselves and make the effort to reframe our thoughts, we strengthen our ability to maintain a more positive, empowering inner dialogue.

In conclusion, reframing negative self-talk is a powerful tool for enhancing our self-esteem and cultivating a healthier, more positive relationship with ourselves. It allows us to challenge our inner critic, replace negative narratives with positive ones, and foster a mindset of self-compassion and understanding. By doing so, we can begin to truly believe that we are enough, just as we are.

## Recognizing Your Strengths

It's a wonderful journey, the exploration of self. You are a complex, multifaceted person, a unique individual with a distinct set of strengths. These strengths, often understated, are the bedrock of your identity, the foundation upon which your life is built. They are the qualities that make you, the real you.

Often, we are so engrossed in our flaws, so consumed by our insecurities, that we overlook our strengths. We tend to focus on our weaknesses, our shortcomings, our failings. This, however, is a skewed perspective, a distorted image of who we truly are. Your strengths are as much a part of you as your weaknesses, and it is important to recognize them, acknowledge them, and celebrate them.

Recognizing your strengths is not about arrogance or self-importance. It's about self-awareness and self-acceptance. It's about understanding that you are enough, just as you are. You don't need to be more, you don't need to be less, you just need to be you.

Your strengths are your tools, your resources. They are the attributes that help you navigate through life, overcome challenges, and achieve your goals. They are the traits that empower you, inspire you, and help you grow. Recognizing your strengths is about identifying these attributes, understanding their value, and utilizing them effectively.

Recognizing your strengths is also about self-love. It's about appreciating yourself, valuing yourself, and honoring yourself. It's about celebrating your achievements, your accomplishments, and your progress. It's about recognizing your worth and believing in your potential. It's about embracing your uniqueness and letting your light shine.

Recognizing your strengths is a journey, a process. It requires introspection, reflection, and self-discovery. It requires courage, honesty, and humility. It requires you to look within, to delve into the depths of your soul, to confront your fears, and to embrace your truth. It requires you to be open, receptive, and accepting. It requires you to be patient, persistent, and resilient.

Recognizing your strengths is empowering. It boosts your confidence, enhances your self-esteem, and strengthens your belief in yourself. It gives you a sense of purpose, a sense of direction, a sense of self. It gives you the courage to pursue your dreams, the determination to overcome your obstacles, and the resilience to bounce back from your setbacks.

Recognizing your strengths is liberating. It frees you from the shackles of self-doubt, self-criticism, and self-deprecation. It frees you from the constraints of societal expectations, cultural norms, and traditional stereotypes. It frees you to be yourself, to express yourself, to love yourself, and to be proud of yourself.

In the end, recognizing your strengths is about embracing your true self. It's about acknowledging your worth, accepting your uniqueness, and celebrating your individuality. It's about understanding that you are enough, just as you are. And always remember, you are more than your weaknesses, more than your flaws, more than your mistakes. You are your strengths, your talents, your passions. You are your hopes, your dreams, your aspirations. You are your courage, your resilience, your perseverance. You are enough. You are more than enough.

## Affirming Your Value

As we journey through life, we often stumble upon the question, "Am I enough?" This question, though small, holds immense power over our self-perception and self-worth. It is a question that makes us doubt our value and worthiness. Yet, the truth is, you are enough. You are more than enough. But to truly embrace this belief, it's important to affirm your value.

Affirming your value isn't about inflating your ego or becoming complacent. To value yourself does not mean that you are so satisfied with your own abilities or situation that you feel you don't need to try any harder. It's about acknowledging your inherent worth and recognizing your unique abilities, talents, and strengths. It is about understanding that your worth is not determined by external factors such as your achievements, possessions, or the approval of others, but by who you are as a person.

It is a common tendency to compare ourselves with others, to measure our worth based on their achievements, their appearances, or their status. But this comparison is a thief of joy; it only leads to feelings of inadequacy and dissatisfaction. Remember, your value does not decrease based on someone's inability to see your worth. You are not a reflection of those who can't recognize your brilliance.

Affirming your value also involves honoring your feelings and emotions. It's okay to feel happy, sad, angry, or scared. Your feelings are valid and they matter. Don't allow anyone to make you feel otherwise. Your feelings are a part of who you are, and they contribute to your unique identity and value.

Self-love and self-care are crucial in affirming your value. Treat yourself with kindness, respect, and compassion. Take care of your physical, mental, and emotional health. When you love and care for yourself, you are affirming your value. You are saying to yourself and to the world, "I matter. I am important. I am worthy."

Affirmations can be powerful tools in affirming your value. Positive self-talk and affirmations can help you change your negative beliefs about yourself and replace them with positive ones. They can help you embrace your worthiness and believe in your potential.

Affirming your value is not a one-time event. It's a continuous process. It's a journey of self-discovery, self-acceptance, and self-love. There will be days when you might find it hard to affirm your value. There will be moments of self-doubt and insecurity. But remember, it's okay. It's part of the journey.

In those moments, remind yourself of your strengths, your accomplishments, and your growth. Remind yourself of the challenges you've overcome and the progress you've made. Remind yourself of the love and kindness you've shown to others. These are the things that define your value, not your mistakes or failures.

Affirming your value is about embracing your imperfectly perfect self. It's about celebrating your uniqueness and individuality. It's about recognizing your worth and believing in your potential.

So, whenever you find yourself questioning, "Am I enough?" remember this: You are enough. You are more than enough. You are valuable. You are worthy. You are deserving of love, respect, and happiness. And no one has the power to make you feel otherwise.

Affirm your value. Believe in yourself. Love yourself. For you are enough, just as you are.

## Nurturing Self-Respect

In the quest for self-discovery and self-appreciation, the cultivation of self-respect is a crucial milestone. This journey is not about vanity or ego; rather, it is about acknowledging your inherent worth and dignity. It's about realizing that you are enough, just as you are.

Self-respect is the cornerstone upon which our self-esteem is built. It is the foundation that allows us to stand tall in the face of adversity, to assert our rights, and to demand fair and respectful treatment from others. It is the quiet confidence that comes from knowing that we are valuable, worthy, and deserving of love and respect.

So, how does one nurture self-respect? It starts with self-awareness. We must develop the ability to observe our thoughts, feelings, and actions without judgment. This mindfulness allows us to recognize our strengths and weaknesses, our achievements, and our shortcomings. It gives us the courage to face our flaws without self-condemnation and to celebrate our victories without arrogance.

Nurturing self-respect also involves setting boundaries. This means learning to say 'no' when necessary and to assert our needs and rights. It means not allowing others to treat us in a way that is disrespectful or demeaning. It means standing up for ourselves, even when it is uncomfortable or difficult.

Self-respect is also about self-care. It's about taking care of our physical, emotional, and mental wellbeing. This includes eating healthy, exercising regularly, getting enough sleep, and taking time for relaxation and recreation. It also involves seeking help when needed, whether it's from a friend, a counselor, or a mental health professional.

Moreover, nurturing self-respect involves practicing self-compassion. We must learn to be kind to ourselves, especially when we make mistakes or face failure. Instead of berating ourselves, we should offer ourselves the same kindness and understanding that we would extend to a friend in a similar situation.

It's also important to remember that self-respect is not about being perfect or meeting unrealistic standards. It's about accepting ourselves as we are, with all our imperfections, and striving to be the best we can be. It's about recognizing our inherent worth, regardless of our achievements, failures, looks, or status.

To nurture self-respect, we must also cultivate a positive mindset. This involves focusing on our strengths instead of our weaknesses, on our achievements instead of our failures. It's about recognizing the good in ourselves and in our lives, even when things are tough.

Lastly, nurturing self-respect requires a commitment to personal growth. This means continuously striving to learn, improve, and become a better person. It means being open to feedback and criticism, and using them as tools for growth rather than as weapons for self-destruction.

In conclusion, nurturing self-respect is an ongoing journey of self-discovery, self-care, and self-improvement. It's about recognizing and affirming our inherent worth and dignity. It's about standing up for ourselves and demanding the respect we deserve. And most importantly, it's about realizing that we are enough, just as we are.

## Building Confidence

In the journey of self-realization and self-acceptance, we often find ourselves standing at the crossroads of self-doubt and confidence. This chapter is dedicated to help you navigate to the path of confidence, a cornerstone to the belief, 'You are Enough'.

To build confidence, it is of paramount importance to first acknowledge that it is not a trait exclusive to a chosen few. It is not a gift, but rather a skill that can be cultivated and nurtured. The seeds of confidence are sown deep within us, waiting patiently to be nurtured and grown.

The first step to building confidence is understanding your self-worth. This involves acknowledging your strengths and weaknesses, embracing your unique characteristics, and valuing your abilities. You are a unique individual with a unique set of skills and talents. No one else in this world can offer what you can. It is essential that you recognize this fact and take pride in it.

Secondly, it is crucial to surround yourself with positivity. The environment you choose to exist in, the people you choose to associate with, and the thoughts you choose to entertain, all play a significant role in shaping your confidence. Positive affirmations and self-talk can be powerful tools in reinforcing confidence.

Remember, failure is not a reflection of your worth. It is merely a stepping stone on your path to success. Every time you stumble, remember that you have the power to rise stronger. This resilience to face failures head-on and learn from them is a crucial factor in building confidence.

Another essential aspect that aids in building confidence is setting realistic and achievable goals. These goals serve as a roadmap guiding you towards your ultimate destination. Achieving these goals not only boosts your confidence but also reinforces your belief in your abilities.

Practice is another essential element in building confidence. The more you practice, the better you become, and the more confident you feel. This applies to all areas of life, whether it is public speaking, writing, playing a sport, or any other skill you wish to master.

Building confidence also involves taking care of your physical health. Regular exercise, a balanced diet, and adequate sleep all contribute to a healthy body and a healthy mind. When you feel good physically, it positively impacts your mental state, thereby boosting your confidence.

Lastly, always remind yourself that you are enough. This mantra is not just a statement, but a belief that you need to reinforce every single day. You are enough, just as you are, with all your imperfections and flaws. You don't need to be more or less of anything to be enough. You don't need anyone or create dependencies to complete yourself. Everything comes later when you are ready to recognize yourself. Every relation will give you happiness when you have discovered your true identity.

Building confidence is not an overnight process. It is a journey, filled with ups and downs, successes and failures. But with each step you take, you are getting closer to becoming the confident person you aspire to be. Remember, the journey is as important as the destination. So, embrace every moment, every challenge, every success, and every failure. They are all contributing to your growth and helping you realize that you are, indeed, enough. All what is required is to trust the process.

Caution: There is a fine line between confidence and overconfidence. How you navigate this line will determine your future success. Overconfidence can stem from underlying insecurities, leading to self-aggrandizement as a cover. True confidence comes from recognizing your abilities while acknowledging areas for growth. Walk this line thoughtfully.

# Chapter 3: Cultivating Self-Love

## Practicing Self-Care

As we embark on this journey of self-realization, we must first acknowledge that, for far too long, we've been neglecting the most important person in our lives: ourselves. For, what good are we to the world if we are not first good to ourselves? This is the essence of self-care, the foundational element of our journey towards embracing the idea that we are indeed enough.

Self-care is not a luxury; it's an absolute necessity. It's a commitment to ourselves that we are worthy, deserving, and enough. We spend so much of our lives catering to the needs and wants of others, often at the expense of our own well-being. We are conditioned to believe that putting ourselves first is selfish, but nothing could be further from the truth. In reality, taking time to nurture our own physical, emotional, and mental health is the most selfless act we can undertake. When we are at our best, we can give our best to those around us.

Practicing self-care involves recognizing our needs and taking steps to meet them. This could mean setting boundaries, saying no when we need to, taking time for relaxation and recreation, eating healthfully, exercising regularly, or seeking professional help when we need it. It's about acknowledging our feelings, allowing ourselves to experience them fully, and then letting them go. It's about understanding that it's okay to not be okay all the time, and that seeking help is not a sign of weakness but a declaration of strength.

Self-care also involves nurturing our minds. This includes engaging in activities that stimulate our intellect, foster creativity, and promote emotional intelligence. It's about challenging our minds, yet also allowing them to rest and recharge. It's about embracing the idea that it's okay to not be busy all the time, and that moments of quiet reflection can be as productive and fulfilling as periods of intense activity.

Perhaps most importantly, self-care is about loving ourselves unconditionally. It's about recognizing our worth, celebrating our strengths, and embracing our flaws. It's about understanding that we are not defined by our mistakes, our failures, or the opinions of others. We are so much more than that. We are unique, valuable, and deserving of love and respect, just as we are.

Self-care is not a destination but a journey. It's a continuous process of learning and growth. It's about constantly reassessing our needs, adjusting our strategies, and being patient with ourselves. It's about understanding that we are works in progress, and that it's okay to not have all the answers.

So, as you turn the pages of this book, remember that the most important relationship you will ever have is the one with yourself. Nurture it, cherish it, and never forget that you are enough. Embrace the practice of self-care and watch as your life transforms in ways you never thought possible. It's not about striving for perfection, but about striving for progress. It's about being kind to yourself, being patient with yourself, and most importantly, loving yourself. Because, at the end of the day, you are enough. Just as you are.

It is advisable to avoid selfishness disguised as self-love. True self-love involves personal growth and betterment, not justifying negative behaviors like laziness, arrogance, anger, manipulation, rebellion, or disrespect. Selfishness masquerading as self-love harms others. As discussed previously, authentic self-love focuses inward on self-improvement, not outward with selfish attitudes.

## Fostering Positive Relationships

As we journey through life, we come to understand that our relationships with others form a significant part of our existence. The connections we make, the bonds we forge, and the interactions we engage in, all contribute to our personal development and growth. As we delve deeper into this chapter, we reflect on the importance and impact of nurturing positive relationships in our lives.

When we talk about relationships, it's not merely confined to romantic relationships. It encapsulates every human connection that we form - family, friends, colleagues, or even strangers. Each relationship holds a mirror to us, reflecting our strengths, flaws, capabilities, and insecurities. They challenge us, comfort us, lift us when we fall, and celebrate with us during our triumphs. Hence, fostering positive relationships becomes essential for our emotional and mental well-being.

But what does a positive relationship look like? It is a connection that thrives on respect, empathy, and understanding. It is a bond that values communication and honesty. It is a tie that encourages growth, offers support, and is rooted in love and compassion. Such relationships nourish our souls, make us feel seen, heard, and appreciated. They remind us that we are enough, just as we are.

Fostering positive relationships, however, does not mean that we must always agree with each other or that conflicts will never arise. Disagreements are a natural part of any relationship. What matters is how we navigate through these disagreements. A positive relationship allows space for healthy debates and discussions, it respects differences and views them as opportunities for learning and growth.

To foster positive relationships, we must first cultivate positivity within ourselves. This starts with self-love and self-acceptance. When we embrace ourselves, with our strengths and flaws, we radiate positivity, which in turn attracts positive relationships. We must remember that we cannot pour from an empty cup. To offer love, respect, and understanding to others, we must first offer these to ourselves.

Active listening is another crucial aspect of positive relationships. It is through listening that we understand the perspectives of others, empathize with their emotions, and respond with kindness and respect. Active listening fosters trust and strengthens the bond between individuals.

Moreover, open and honest communication forms the backbone of positive relationships. It involves expressing our thoughts and emotions without fear of judgment and being receptive to the thoughts and feelings of others. It is through such communication that misunderstandings are cleared, conflicts are resolved, and relationships are strengthened.

In addition, practicing gratitude can enhance our relationships. When we appreciate the people in our lives and express our gratitude towards them, it not only makes them feel valued but also deepens our connection with them.

Lastly, it is important to remember that fostering positive relationships is a continuous journey, not a destination. It requires effort, patience, and understanding. It involves setting boundaries, respecting them, and honoring the boundaries set by others. It entails celebrating the uniqueness of each individual and embracing the diversity of thoughts, opinions, and experiences.

As we reflect upon these insights, let us strive to foster positive relationships in our lives. Let us remember that each relationship is a unique tapestry woven with threads of unconditional love, respect, understanding, and empathy. And above all, let us remind ourselves that we are enough, just as we are.

## Setting Healthy Boundaries

In this journey of self-discovery and self-love, we must not overlook a crucial aspect: setting healthy boundaries. This is not just about demarcating our physical space but also our emotional, mental, and spiritual territories. It is about defining what we are comfortable with, what we can tolerate, and what we absolutely cannot. It is about understanding our limits and not permitting others to cross them. Not out of malice or selfishness, but out of respect and care for our own well-being.

Boundaries are not walls. They do not shut us off from the world but rather, they protect our inner sanctum from unnecessary harm. They act as filters, allowing in only what aligns with our values, beliefs, and personal comfort. They are not rigid, unyielding barriers but flexible lines that can be adjusted as we grow and change.

Healthy boundaries are an extension of self-love. They are a way of saying, "I value myself enough to not let anyone or anything harm me." They are a way of asserting our worth, of affirming that we are, indeed, enough. But how do we go about setting these boundaries?

The first step is self-awareness. We must know ourselves well enough to understand what we need from our relationships and interactions. We must be aware of our emotional responses, our triggers, and our breaking points. We must be in tune with our feelings and respect them enough to give them voice.

The next step is communication. Once we know our boundaries, we need to express them clearly and assertively. This does not mean being aggressive or confrontational. It simply means stating our needs and expectations without guilt or apology. It might be uncomfortable at first, especially if we are not used to speaking up for ourselves, but with practice, it becomes easier.

The third step is consistency. Setting boundaries is not a one-time act. It is a continuous process that needs to be maintained and reinforced. It is not enough to state our boundaries; we must also uphold them. If people disregard our boundaries, we need to remind them and, if necessary, distance ourselves from them. This might seem harsh, but it is essential for our mental and emotional health.

Setting healthy boundaries might seem daunting, but it is an empowering act. It is a declaration of our independence and a testament to our self-worth. It is a way of taking control of our lives and steering them in the direction we want.

However, it is also important to remember that boundaries are not just about protecting ourselves. They are also about respecting others. Just as we have the right to set our boundaries, others have the right to set theirs. It is a two-way street that requires understanding, respect, and mutual consent.

In conclusion, setting healthy boundaries is an integral part of self-love and self-respect. It is about recognizing and honoring our worth. It is about asserting our right to be treated with respect and decency. It is about standing up for ourselves and saying, "I am enough, and I deserve to be treated as such." It is not always easy, but it is always worth it. Because we are worth it. We are more than enough.

## Honoring Your Feelings

As we continue our journey of self-discovery and acceptance, it is paramount to acknowledge the importance of our emotions. Our feelings are a compass, guiding us through the labyrinth of life, signaling when we are aligned with our true selves or when we are straying from our path. They are not obstacles to be overcome, but rather valuable tools to be understood and honored.

Often, we are taught to suppress our emotions, to put on a brave face, to keep our feelings guarded. But emotions are not signs of weakness; they are part of our human experience. They are our body's way of communicating with us, of telling us something about ourselves or our situation. They are the raw, unfiltered expression of our inner selves, and they deserve to be acknowledged and respected.

To honor our feelings means to give them the space they need to exist, to be felt, to be understood. It means not rushing to judgment or dismissal, but rather approaching them with curiosity and compassion. It means allowing them to flow through us, to express themselves, without trying to control or manipulate them.

It's important to recognize that honoring our feelings does not mean being ruled by them. It does not mean acting impulsively or recklessly based on how we feel in the moment. Rather, it means acknowledging our emotions as valid and significant, and then making conscious choices about how to respond to them.

Honoring our feelings begins with awareness. We need to become aware of what we are feeling, why we are feeling it, and how it is affecting us. This requires us to tune into our bodies, to pay attention to our physical sensations, our thoughts, and our behaviors. It requires us to slow down, to be present with ourselves, to listen to our inner voice.

Once we are aware of our feelings, we can begin to understand them. We can ask ourselves: What is this emotion trying to tell me? What is it reflecting about my beliefs, my values, my needs? How can I use this information to better understand myself and my situation?

Finally, honoring our feelings means expressing them in healthy and constructive manner. This could mean having a difficult conversation, setting a boundary, seeking support, or simply allowing ourselves to cry, to laugh, to feel. It means not bottling up our emotions, but letting them out in ways that honor our truth and our dignity. Choosing to become angry or rebellious is simply a question of expression; nevertheless, decisions can be taken and emotions may be expressed far more peacefully when it comes to most situations.

Remember, our feelings are not good or bad, right or wrong. They simply are. And they are part of who we are. By honoring our feelings, we honor ourselves. We affirm that we matter, that our experiences matter, that our emotions matter. We affirm that we are enough, just as we are.

In the end, honoring our feelings is an act of self-love. It is a way of saying: I see you. I hear you. I respect you. I love you. It is a way of embracing our whole selves, emotions and all, and declaring: You are enough. And always will be.

## Embracing Self-Compassion

In the journey towards self-acceptance, it is vital to cultivate a habit of self-compassion. This is not just about being gentle with yourself; it is about acknowledging your human frailties and understanding they do not diminish your worth. It is about enveloping yourself in a cocoon of kindness, even in moments of failure and disappointment. This is the essence of self-compassion.

Self-compassion is the soothing balm that heals the wounds inflicted by harsh self-judgment. It is the voice that whispers, "it's okay" when you stumble and fall. It is the gentle hand that picks you up, dusts you off and encourages you to try again. It is the ability to recognize that you are enough, just as you are, with your imperfections and shortcomings.

But embracing self-compassion is not always easy. In a world that constantly pushes us towards perfection, it can be challenging to show kindness to ourselves. We are often our own harshest critics, berating ourselves for the smallest mistakes, blaming ourselves for things beyond our control, and setting unrealistic expectations that leave us feeling inadequate.

However, the transformative power of self-compassion cannot be underestimated. It is a powerful tool that can significantly alter your perception of self-worth. It allows you to view your mistakes as opportunities for growth rather than markers of failure. It encourages you to treat yourself with the same kindness and understanding you would extend to a loved one in distress.

Embracing self-compassion requires a conscious shift in mindset. It requires you to challenge the negative self-talk and replace it with words of kindness. It requires you to practice patience with yourself, to understand that growth is a process and that it's okay to take your time. It requires you to realize that you are not alone in your struggles, that everyone experiences moments of self-doubt and insecurity.

Self-compassion also involves taking care of your physical wellbeing. Your body is your vessel in this world, and it deserves to be treated with respect and care. Eating well, exercising regularly, getting enough sleep - these are all acts of self-compassion. They are ways of saying to yourself, "I am worth taking care of."

The beauty of self-compassion is that it is a skill that can be learned and cultivated. It is not a trait that you either have or don't have. It is a practice that requires dedication and consistency. Just like a muscle, it strengthens with regular use.

As you journey towards embracing self-compassion, remember that it is not a destination but a continuous process. There will be days when it will be harder to be kind to yourself, but those are the days when you need self-compassion the most.

By embracing self-compassion, you are not only nurturing a healthier relationship with yourself, but you are also setting the foundation for healthier relationships with others. After all, how we treat ourselves often reflects how we treat others.

In conclusion, self-compassion is not a sign of weakness or self-indulgence. It is a testament to your strength, resilience, and understanding. It is a celebration of your humanity. It is an acknowledgment that you are, indeed, enough. So, embrace self-compassion and let it guide you towards a more fulfilling and contented life.

# Chapter 4: Pursuing Personal Growth

## Setting Personal Goals

In the journey of self-discovery and personal development, a definitive compass to guide us is the establishment of personal goals. They serve not just as a roadmap, but also as a mirror, reflecting our deepest desires, ambitions and the person we aspire to be. They are the whispers of our soul, the echoes of our hearts, serving as a constant reminder that we are enough, and we have the potential to be more.

Personal goals are a manifestation of our self-worth and self-belief. They are the tangible expressions of our belief in our capacity to grow, to learn, and to achieve. They are the milestones we set for ourselves, the landmarks that guide us on our journey of self-improvement. They help us measure our progress, evaluate our strategies, and make necessary adjustments to our course. They are the stepping stones that lead us towards our ultimate goal – the realization of our fullest potential.

The process of setting personal goals is a deeply introspective one. It begins with a thorough examination and understanding of ourselves - our strengths, our weaknesses, our passions, and our aspirations. This self-awareness forms the foundation for our goals. It helps us identify the areas we need to work on, the skills we need to develop, and the habits we need to cultivate. It gives us a clear picture of where we are, where we want to go, and the steps we need to take to get there.

Setting personal goals also involves a fair amount of introspection and self-reflection. It requires us to look within, to confront our fears, to challenge our limitations, and to question our assumptions. It compels us to step out of our comfort zones, to take risks, and to push our boundaries. It encourages us to dream, to aspire, and to strive.

The beauty of personal goals is that they are, by definition, personal. They are not dictated by societal norms, expectations, or pressures. They are not influenced by the achievements or failures of others. They are unique to us, reflecting our individuality and uniqueness. They resonate with our personal values, align with our passions, and are fueled by our innermost desires.

However, setting personal goals is not enough. We must also be committed to achieving them. This requires discipline, determination, and resilience. It requires us to persevere in the face of challenges, to persist in the face of setbacks, and to remain focused in the face of distractions. It requires us to be proactive, to take initiative, and to take responsibility for our actions.

In the end, the ultimate goal is not the achievement of our personal goals, but the person we become in the process. The skills we develop, the knowledge we gain, and the experiences we accumulate along the way are far more valuable than the goals themselves. They shape our character, enrich our lives, and enhance our sense of self-worth. They remind us, time and again, that we are enough.

Setting personal goals is a journey of self-discovery, self-improvement, and self-fulfillment. It is a journey that challenges us, inspires us, and empowers us. It is a journey that reminds us of our potential, our worth, and our capacity to achieve. It is a journey that reaffirms our belief in ourselves, and in the power of our dreams.

## Embracing Change

In the journey of self-discovery and acceptance, one of the most significant challenges we encounter is change. It is an inevitable part of life, yet it often stirs up feelings of fear and uncertainty. But what if we could shift our perspective and see change not as a threat, but as a catalyst for growth?

Change can be uncomfortable. It disrupts our routines, our comfort zones, and our expectations. But it is in this discomfort that we are given the opportunity to evolve, to learn, and to expand our horizons. Change can be the key that unlocks our potential and brings us closer to the realization that we are enough.

As we tread on our path, we must remember that change is not a measure of inadequacy. It does not imply that we were insufficient before or that we need to be different to be worthy. Instead, change is a testament to our capacity for growth. It is an indication to our resilience and adaptability. It is a testament to our innate potential to evolve and flourish in the face of life's many twists and turns.

Embracing change is about more than just accepting its inevitability. It's about embracing the uncertainty and unpredictability that comes with it. It's about seeing the unknown not as a source of fear, but as a realm of endless possibilities. It's about understanding that our growth is not linear, and that's okay. It's about recognizing that even when we stumble and fall, we are still enough.

When we resist change, we resist growth. We remain stuck in our old ways, trapped by our fears and insecurities. But when we embrace change, we open ourselves up to new experiences, new perspectives, and new opportunities. We allow ourselves to grow, to learn, and to become the best versions of ourselves.

But embracing change is not always easy. It requires courage, resilience, and a lot of self-compassion. It requires us to let go of our need for control, to face our fears head-on, and to trust in our ability to navigate through the unknown. It requires us to be patient with ourselves, to acknowledge our feelings, and to give ourselves the grace to stumble and fall.

However, the beauty of embracing change is that it allows us to discover parts of ourselves that we might not have known existed. It helps us to uncover our strengths, our passions, and our values. It helps us to understand that we are not defined by our past or our circumstances, but by our capacity for growth and transformation.

In the face of change, we are reminded that we are not static beings. We are dynamic, ever-evolving, and capable of immense growth. We are reminded that we are not defined by a single moment or a single mistake, but by our journey and our capacity to learn and grow from our experiences.

Embracing change is an act of self-love. It is a commitment to our growth and well-being. It is an affirmation of our worthiness and our potential. It is a reminder that we are enough, just as we are, and that we will continue to be enough, no matter how much we change and grow.

So, as you navigate through the ebbs and flows of life, remember to embrace change. Remember that it is a part of your journey, a part of your growth, and a part of you. Remember that you are enough, and always will be.

## Overcoming Challenges

As we journey through the labyrinth of life, we are often confronted with hurdles that seem insurmountable. These challenges, though daunting, are not walls meant to halt our progress, but rather stepping stones designed to propel us to greater heights. In the grand scheme of life, they are instrumental in shaping our character and defining our path.

In my own life, I've encountered various challenges that have tested my mettle and resolve. I've faced moments of self-doubt, despair, and the overwhelming feeling of being insufficient. It was in these moments that I discovered the power of self-belief and the profound truth that I am enough.

The first step to overcoming challenges is acknowledging them. We often tend to avoid or escape our problems, hoping they would somehow disappear. However, this only leads to amplified stress and anxiety. Instead, we should confront these difficulties head-on, understanding that they are a part of life's journey. Acknowledging our challenges does not mean succumbing to them; rather, it means accepting their existence and preparing to tackle them.

Once we have acknowledged our challenges, it's essential to maintain a positive mindset. It's natural to feel overwhelmed and defeated when faced with adversity. However, a positive mindset can significantly influence our ability to overcome these obstacles. It's important to remember that our thoughts shape our reality. If we believe we can overcome, we are already halfway there.

But how do you maintain positivity amidst adversity? It's all about perspective. We need to shift our focus from the problem itself to potential solutions. Instead of dwelling on how big our problems are, we should focus on how we can use them to grow and evolve. This shift in perspective can significantly change our approach to challenges.

Another key aspect of overcoming challenges is resilience. Life won't always go as planned, and we might stumble and fall. However, the ability to get back up and continue pushing forward is what truly defines us. Resilience is not about never falling; it's about getting up each time we fall.

In my journey, I've found that self-love and self-care play a crucial role in overcoming challenges. We often tend to be our harshest critics, focusing on our failures rather than our successes. We focus on what we don't have instead of what we have in our plate. However, it's crucial to remember that we are human, and it's okay to make mistakes. What's important is to learn from these mistakes and use them as stepping stones towards our goals.

Lastly, remember to celebrate every victory, no matter how small. Every step forward, every challenge overcome, is a testament to your strength and resilience. Celebrating these victories not only boosts our morale but also reinforces our belief in our capabilities.

In conclusion, overcoming challenges is not about eliminating adversity from our lives. It's about embracing these challenges and using them to grow and evolve. It's about believing in our strength, resilience, and ability to overcome. And most importantly, it's about loving ourselves through the process, understanding that we are not defined by our challenges, but how we rise above them.

## Learning From Mistakes

As we traverse the journey of life, there are moments when we feel the sting of failure, the bitter taste of a mistake. It is a universal experience, one that transcends cultures and societies, an inevitable part of our existence. However, it is also within these moments of seeming defeat that we find our greatest potential for growth and self-discovery.

Often, we are conditioned to view mistakes as negative, as signs of inadequacy. We are taught to strive for perfection, to avoid errors at all costs. Yet, this mindset overlooks the inherent value in our missteps. In reality, mistakes are not indictments of our worth, but opportunities for learning and growth. They are signposts, pointing us towards areas in which we can improve and develop.

Each mistake is a lesson in disguise, an invitation to examine our actions and decisions, to reflect on our motivations and desires. When we make a mistake, it serves as a mirror, reflecting back to us aspects of ourselves that we may have overlooked or ignored. It is a wake-up call, reminding us of our humanity, our fallibility, and our potential.

Consider this: every mistake is a step on the path to self-discovery. Each error, each misstep, each failure is a stepping stone, a bridge that leads us closer to our true selves. Mistakes force us to confront our weaknesses, to face our fears, and to challenge our assumptions. They compel us to question, to seek, and to grow.

Moreover, mistakes help us cultivate resilience, perseverance, and courage. They teach us to pick ourselves up after a fall, to dust off the dirt, and to keep moving forward. They remind us that it's okay to stumble, it's okay to falter, and it's okay to not have all the answers. In fact, it's more than okay; it's necessary.

When we learn to see our mistakes as teachers rather than tormentors, we begin to embrace them. We stop running from them, stop fearing them. Instead, we welcome them as guides on our path to self-improvement. We start to view them as stepping stones rather than stumbling blocks.

However, learning from our mistakes requires honesty and humility. It requires us to shed the layers of denial, defensiveness, and self-deception. It demands that we look at ourselves in the mirror and accept our flaws and failings. It necessitates that we take responsibility for our actions and decisions, that we own up to our mistakes.

In the grand scheme of things, mistakes are not the end of the world. They are not a mark of shame or a sign of incompetence. They are simply part of the human experience, part of the journey of growth and self-discovery.

So, the next time you make a mistake, do not berate yourself or wallow in self-pity. Instead, take a step back, take a deep breath, and view it as an opportunity to learn, to grow, and to improve. Remember, it's not about how many times you fall, but how many times you pick yourself up.

In the end, our mistakes do not define us. It is how we respond to them, how we learn from them, that truly shapes our character and our destiny. So, embrace your mistakes, learn from them, and remember: you are enough. Just as you are.

## Celebrating Success

In our journey of self-discovery and personal growth, acknowledging and celebrating our achievements, no matter how small, is essential. It is through these moments of victory that we reaffirm to ourselves that we are indeed enough. This chapter is dedicated to celebrating success, a crucial aspect that often gets overshadowed in our relentless pursuit of perfection.

Success isn't always about grand achievements or monumental victories. Sometimes, it's about recognizing the little things, the small steps we take towards our goals. When we celebrate these small victories, we fuel our motivation and nurture our self-esteem. We affirm our abilities and capabilities, assuring ourselves that we are on the right path. This is the essence of celebrating success, not as an end goal, but as a part of the journey.

Often, we fall into the trap of comparing our success to others. We measure our achievements based on what others have accomplished, leading to feelings of inadequacy and self-doubt. But remember, success is not a competition. It is a personal journey, unique to each individual. Celebrating success is about acknowledging your own progress, not comparing it to someone else's.

It's important to understand that success is relative. What may seem like a small feat to someone might be a significant achievement for another. Maybe you finally managed to wake up early in the morning, read a book you've been putting off for months, or even just stood up for yourself in a difficult situation. These are all successes worth celebrating.

Celebrating success also fosters a positive mindset. When we acknowledge our achievements, we are essentially focusing on the positive aspects of our lives. This helps to cultivate an attitude of gratitude and positivity, which in turn enhances our overall mental and emotional well-being.

However, celebrating success doesn't mean we should become complacent. It's not about settling for less or stopping after achieving a goal. Instead, it's about taking a moment to appreciate the progress we've made, using it as a stepping stone to strive for even greater heights. It's about acknowledging that we are enough, but we can always become more.

As we celebrate our successes, it's also important to remember the struggles and failures that led us to them. Success isn't a straight path; it's a winding road filled with obstacles and setbacks. It's about learning from our mistakes, growing from our failures, and using them as stepping stones to success. In this sense, even our failures are worth celebrating, for they are what shape us into the people we are.

In conclusion, celebrating success is about more than just acknowledging our achievements. It's about reaffirming our worth, nurturing our self-esteem, and fostering a positive mindset. It's about recognizing that we are enough, and yet, we can always strive for more. So, celebrate your successes, big or small, for they are the milestones in your journey of self-discovery and personal growth.

Remember, you are enough. You have always been enough. And as you continue to grow and succeed, you will realize that you are more than enough. In the end, the journey matters more than the destination. So, take a moment to celebrate your success, for you have earned it.

# Chapter 5: Harnessing Your Potential

## Unleashing Your Creativity

Embrace the notion that creativity isn't a rare gift to be enjoyed by the lucky few, but a natural part of human thinking and behavior. In truth, we are all brimming with curiosity, the ability to solve problems, the capacity to make connections between unrelated things, and the power to imagine what might be. It's a matter of acknowledging this inherent capability and giving it the space to flourish.

Our creativity is often stifled by fear – fear of failure, fear of the unknown, fear of judgment. We worry about messing up, about not being good enough, or about being perceived as weird or different. These fears can be so powerful that they hinder us from expressing our true selves and realizing our full potential. Yet, to open the gates to your creativity, you must learn to overcome these fears. Remember, there is no right or wrong in the realm of creativity. It's all about exploration, experimentation, and expression.

To unleash your creativity, start by changing your mindset. Instead of viewing creativity as a fixed trait, see it as a muscle that can be strengthened with regular exercise. This shift in perspective can make a significant difference. It can free you from the constraints of perfectionism and the fear of making mistakes, enabling you to take risks, make bold decisions, and try new things.

Next, cultivate a sense of curiosity. Be open to new experiences, ideas, and perspectives. Ask questions, seek answers, and strive to understand the world from different viewpoints. Remember, creativity often stems from curiosity. It's about asking "What if?" and being willing to explore the possibilities.

Furthermore, embrace failure as part of the creative process. Every mistake, every failure, is an opportunity to learn and grow. Instead of being discouraged by failure, see it as a stepping stone towards success. It's through making mistakes that we discover new ways of doing things, uncover hidden potentials, and learn valuable lessons.

In addition, surround yourself with diverse influences. Seek inspiration from various sources – books, movies, music, nature, people, cultures, and experiences. The more diverse your influences, the more raw material you have for creative thinking. It's in the intersection of these different influences that unique and innovative ideas often emerge.

Practice mindfulness- Be present in the moment. Observe your surroundings. Listen to your thoughts and feelings. Mindfulness can enhance your creativity by helping you notice details, make connections, and generate new ideas.

Lastly, create a conducive environment for creativity. This could be a physical space filled with things that inspire you or a mental space where you feel safe, relaxed, and free to express yourself. It could also be a social environment that encourages diversity, collaboration, and open-mindedness.

Unleashing your creativity isn't about becoming the next Picasso or Mozart. It's about expressing yourself, solving problems, generating new ideas, and making your life and the world around you more interesting and vibrant. It's about realizing that you are enough, that you have what it takes to create, innovate, and make a difference. The age does not determine creativity. All you have to do is explore your hobbies to start over.

In the end, creativity isn't a destination, but a journey – a journey of self-discovery, personal growth, and endless possibilities. So, embark on this journey. Unleash your creativity. And see where it takes you.

## Maximizing Your Skills

In the journey of self-discovery and self-affirmation, it is crucial to recognize and maximize your skills. This process is not simply about listing your abilities; it is a profound exploration of your inner strengths, the unique talents that set you apart from the rest. Remember, you are enough, and your skills, however simple they may seem, are your tools for making a difference in your life and the world.

The first step to maximizing your skills is acknowledging them. Often, we downplay our abilities or fail to see them as valuable. This self-deprecating attitude can hinder our growth and self-acceptance. Understand that every skill you possess, be it communication, creative thinking, problem-solving, or empathy, is significant and worth celebrating. Embrace these skills, for they are integral parts of who you are.

Next, it's time to refine these skills. Just as a diamond need cutting and polishing to reveal its brilliance, your skills need honing to reach their full potential. This may involve training, practice, or stepping out of your comfort zone. Embrace the process with patience and persistence, knowing that every effort you make contributes to your growth.

Maximizing your skills also involves application. A skill unused is like a bird with clipped wings – unable to soar to great heights. Use your skills in your daily life, at work, or in pursuit of your passions. Not only will this allow you to experience the joy and fulfillment of utilizing your abilities, but it also provides opportunities for further growth and learning.

Moreover, don't hesitate to share your skills with others. Teaching is a powerful way to reinforce what you know and to gain a deeper understanding of your skills. In sharing, you also inspire others to recognize and develop their skills, creating a ripple effect of growth and empowerment.

It is equally important to remain open to learning new skills. The world is an endless source of knowledge and experiences, and every new skill you acquire adds to your unique cluster of abilities. Embrace the learner within you, knowing that every new skill is a testament to your capacity for growth and adaptation.

Lastly, remember to appreciate your skills. In a world that often values competition over personal growth, it's easy to compare our abilities with others and feel inadequate. Resist this urge. Your skills are not meant to be compared but to be celebrated. They are your personal treasures, testament to your individuality and potential.

Maximizing your skills is not a one-time event but a lifelong journey. It requires self-awareness, dedication, and above all, self-love. Remember that each skill you possess is a reflection of your uniqueness, your strength, and your potential. They are your tools for creating a life of purpose, fulfillment, and joy.

So, embrace your skills, maximize them, and let them shine. Because you are enough, and your skills are the unique colors that make up the beautiful masterpiece that is you.

## Expressing Your Passions

As we travel through life's fabric, we find ourselves woven into a myriad of experiences, each thread colored by our passions. It is these passions that ignite the flame within us, fueling our existence with a sense of purpose and joy. But how often do we truly express these passions? How often do we allow ourselves the freedom to be completely consumed by what sets our souls on fire?

Often, we suppress our passions, tucking them away in the corners of our hearts. We believe that the world might not understand, or worse, might judge or ridicule us. We fear that our passions may not align with societal expectations or that they may not provide us with a stable future. We tend to forget that we are enough, with our unique blend of interests and passions.

Every passion, no matter how small or seemingly insignificant, holds within it a spark of our truest selves. It is an echo of our innermost desires, a whisper of our authentic selves. When we express our passions, we are not just sharing a hobby or an interest. We are sharing a piece of our soul, a fragment of our identity.

Expressing our passions is not merely about verbalizing them. It is about living them, immersing ourselves in them, and allowing them to radiate from our being. It is about finding the courage to dance even when the world is watching, to paint even when the canvas is intimidating, to write even when the words seem elusive. It is about daring to dream, daring to hope, and daring to love what we do with fervor and intensity.

Expressing our passions is also about sharing them with others. It is about inspiring and being inspired, about learning and teaching, about giving and receiving. It is about creating a space where our passions can flourish and grow, where they can touch lives and make a difference.

Yet, it is crucial to remember that our worth is not defined by our passions. We are not less worthy if our passions do not align with conventional standards of success or if they do not result in tangible outcomes. Our passions are not a measure of our worth; they are a celebration of our uniqueness, a testament to our individuality.

Embracing our passions requires us to confront our fears and insecurities. It requires us to step out of our comfort zones and face the unknown. It requires us to be vulnerable, to expose our hearts and souls to the world. But in doing so, we find our truest selves. We find joy, fulfillment, and a sense of purpose.

So, let us not shy away from expressing our passions. Let us wear them proudly, like badges of honor. Let us paint the canvas of our lives with the vibrant colors of our passions, creating a masterpiece that is uniquely ours.

Remember, you are enough. Your passions are enough. They are an integral part of who you are, and they deserve to be celebrated. So, express your passions. Live them. Share them. And in doing so, let the world see the radiant, passionate, and authentic you.

## Envisioning Your Future

As we traverse the path of our lives, it is crucial to remember that the journey is as much about the future as it is about the present. This journey isn't just about accepting and loving who we are now, but it also involves embracing who we could become. Therefore, this chapter invites you to envision your future, to dream, and to explore the possibilities that lie ahead.

Envisioning your future can be both an exhilarating and daunting task. It's like standing at the edge of a vast ocean, knowing that you're about to embark on a journey into the unknown. Yet, in this uncertainty lies the magic of possibilities. You have the power to shape your future, to steer the course of your life in the direction you desire.

Consider your dreams, hopes, and aspirations. What does your ideal future look like? Who do you see yourself becoming? In taking the time to contemplate these questions, you are allowing yourself to step into a realm of limitless potential. You are giving yourself permission to dream and to aspire for more.

But while it's important to dream, it's equally important to ground these dreams in reality. This doesn't mean limiting yourself or being pessimistic. Instead, it means understanding that while the future holds infinite possibilities, achieving your dreams requires action, commitment, and resilience.

When envisioning your future, remember to be kind to yourself. Your future doesn't have to be grand or extravagant to be meaningful. Instead, it should be a reflection of your values, passions, and desires. It should be a future where you can say with certainty, "I am enough."

It's also important to remember that the future is not set in stone. The path you envision for yourself today may change as you grow and evolve. And that's okay. Life is not about following a straight, predetermined path. It's about exploration, growth, and continual self-discovery.

When you envision your future, you are not just planning. You are also manifesting. You are projecting your desires into the universe, setting the stage for them to come to fruition. Therefore, be bold in your dreams. Be daring in your aspirations. Let your future be as vast, as diverse, and as beautiful as you are.

As you embark on this journey of envisioning your future, remember to carry with you the knowledge of your inherent worth. You are enough, just as you are. You are enough, in your dreams and your aspirations. You are enough, in your journey towards your envisioned future.

This journey of envisioning your future is a testament to your courage and your faith in yourself. It's an affirmation of your worth and your potential. So, dream. Aspire. Strive. For in doing so, you are not just shaping your future. You are also shaping your present, making it a testament to your strength, your resilience, and your unwavering belief in your own worth.

So, as you stand at the edge of that vast ocean, ready to embark on the journey towards your envisioned future, remember this: You are enough. You are more than enough. And the future you envision for yourself, the future you strive for, is a future that you are wholly and completely worthy of.

## Achieving Your Dreams

As we journey through life, we often find ourselves standing at the precipice of our dreams, gazing out at the seemingly insurmountable expanse that separates us from them. The chasm between where we are and where we aspire to be can be daunting, but it's essential to remember that you, as you are, are enough to traverse it.

Every dream, regardless of its size or complexity, begins with a single step. This step, often daunting, is the first leap of faith you take towards your dreams. It's a declaration to yourself and the universe that you are ready and willing to pursue what your heart yearns for. Remember, this step doesn't have to be monumental. It can be as simple as writing down your goals, enrolling in a class, or even just verbalizing your dreams to someone else. The important thing is that you're taking action, however small.

Next, it's crucial to understand that dreams don't materialize overnight. They require time, effort, and persistence. There will be days when you feel like your progress is slow, and you might even question whether your dreams are attainable. During these moments, it's essential to remember why you started. Recalling your reasons can reignite your passion and provide the motivation you need to keep moving forward.

Moreover, achieving your dreams often requires stepping outside of your comfort zone. This can be intimidating and can sometimes lead to self-doubt. However, it's crucial to remember that growth often happens when we're uncomfortable. It's in these moments of discomfort that we learn more about ourselves and our capabilities. Always remember, you have everything you need within you to overcome these challenges.

To achieve your dreams, you must also be willing to fail. Failure is often seen as a negative outcome, but it's actually a valuable learning experience. Each failure brings you one step closer to your dreams by teaching you what doesn't work and pushing you to find what does. So, don't be afraid to fail. Embrace it, learn from it, and use it as a stepping stone towards your dreams.

Finally, achieving your dreams requires a strong belief in yourself. You must believe that you are capable, worthy, and enough to achieve your dreams. This belief acts as a self-fulfilling prophecy. When you believe in yourself, you empower yourself to take the necessary steps towards your dreams. You ask the cosmos to help you realize your full potential and become one of a kind.

In conclusion, achieving your dreams is a journey that requires action, persistence, courage, a willingness to fail, and a strong belief in oneself. It can be a challenging journey, filled with ups and downs. Always keep in mind that you possess everything necessary to embark on this journey. You have an abundance of strength, courage, and wisdom within you, as you are the one chosen for this life's expedition. So, take that first step, keep going, believe in yourself, and watch as you turn your dreams into reality.

# Chapter 6: Inspiring Others

## Living By Example

In our journey through life, we often find ourselves playing the roles of both student and teacher. We learn from our experiences, our mistakes, and others around us, and in turn, we impart our wisdom and knowledge to those who cross our paths. It's a continuous cycle of learning and teaching, of receiving and giving. However, we often underestimate the profound impact we can have on others, especially when we are not consciously trying to teach or guide. This is where the concept of 'Living by Example' comes into play.

Living by example is not just about being a good person; it's about being your authentic self. It's about embracing who you are, with all your flaws and strengths, and living your life in a way that aligns with your values and beliefs. It's about embodying your principles, not just preaching them. It's about leading with actions, not words. It's about showing others that it's okay to be imperfect, to make mistakes, to be vulnerable, to ask for help, to be different. It's about showing them that they are enough, just as they are.

When we live by example, we inadvertently become role models for others. We might not even realize it, but our actions and behaviors can have a profound impact on those around us. They can inspire, motivate, and influence others in ways we might never even imagine. Our actions can give others the courage to embrace their uniqueness, to overcome their fears, to pursue their dreams, to stand up for what they believe in, to be kind to themselves and others.

However, living by example is not always easy. It requires courage, honesty, and integrity. It requires us to be true to ourselves and our values, even when it's uncomfortable or challenging. It requires us to face our fears, to confront our weaknesses, to accept our flaws, to forgive ourselves and others. It requires us to take responsibility for our actions and their consequences. It requires us to be mindful of our words and actions, knowing that they can influence others.

Moreover, living by example is not about being perfect. It's about being real, being human. It's about showing others that it's okay to have bad days, to struggle, to not have all the answers. It's about showing them that it's okay to be a work in progress, that it's okay to grow and evolve, that it's okay to be imperfectly perfect. It's about showing them that they don't have to be perfect to be enough.

In conclusion, living by example is a powerful way to influence and inspire others. It's a way to lead with authenticity, integrity, and courage. It's a way to show others that they are enough, just as they are. So let's strive to live by example, not just for ourselves, but for those around us. Let's strive to be the change we wish to see in the world. Let's strive to be the person we would want to look up to. Let's strive to be enough, just as we are.

## Building Meaningful Connections

In our journey of self-discovery and self-love, it is not just enough to understand and appreciate our own worth, but also to recognize the value of others and build meaningful connections with them. Relationships are the threads that weave the tapestry of our lives, adding color, texture, and depth to our existence. They shape us, influence us, and in many ways, define us. However, nurturing these connections requires a delicate balance of giving and receiving, understanding, compassion and empathy.

The essence of building meaningful connections lies in the authenticity of our interactions. Genuine relationships are not built on pretenses or superficialities; they thrive on transparency, sincerity, and mutual respect. To foster such relationships, we must first be true to ourselves. When we accept ourselves as we are, with our strengths and weaknesses, we are more likely to extend the same acceptance to others. This mutual acceptance forms the bedrock of a meaningful connection.

However, accepting ourselves and others is only the first step. Communication is the bridge that connects two souls, facilitating understanding and empathy. Open, honest, and respectful communication is the cornerstone of any strong relationship. It is through communication that we express our thoughts, feelings, and perspectives, and understand those of others. In a world where digital communication often replaces face-to-face interactions, it is important to remember the value of personal, heartfelt conversations.

Yet, communication is not just about speaking; it is equally about listening. Listening is an act of love, a gift we give to others. When we truly listen to another person, we show them that we value their thoughts and feelings. We make them feel seen, heard, and understood. Active listening involves not just hearing the words someone is saying, but also understanding the emotions behind those words. It requires empathy, patience, and a genuine interest in the other person's experiences.

At the same time, building meaningful connections is not a one-size-fits-all process. Each relationship is unique, shaped by the individual personalities, experiences, and perspectives of the people involved. What works in one relationship may not work in another. Therefore, it is important to be flexible and adaptable, to respect the individuality of the other person, and to be willing to learn and grow together.

Moreover, meaningful connections are not limited to our personal lives. They extend to our professional lives as well. In a world where competition often overshadows collaboration, it is important to remember the value of teamwork and mutual support. By building strong, respectful, and supportive relationships in the workplace, we can create a positive, productive environment that benefits everyone involved.

Finally, it is important to remember that building meaningful connections takes time. It requires effort, patience, and commitment. But the rewards are well worth the effort. The joy of shared experiences, the comfort of mutual understanding, the growth that comes from shared learning – these are the treasures that meaningful connections bring into our lives.

In conclusion, building meaningful connections is an integral part of our journey towards self-love and self-acceptance. By being true to ourselves, communicating openly, listening actively, respecting individuality, and committing to the process, we can build relationships that enrich our lives and help us become the best versions of ourselves. Remember, you are enough, and you have the capacity to build meaningful, fulfilling connections with others.

## Sharing Your Story

Stepping into the realm of vulnerability, we begin to unravel the power of sharing one's story. As we traverse the path of life, every individual crafts a one-of-a-kind masterpiece woven with personal encounters, victories, and setbacks. Embracing the courage to share our narratives not only liberates us, but also has the potential to inspire and resonate with others.

In the grand scheme of life, our stories are the footprints we leave behind. They are the echoes of our existence, reverberating through time and space. Each story is a testament to our resilience, a celebration of our victories, and a poignant reminder of our shared humanity.

As we delve into the art of storytelling, it's crucial to remember that the act of sharing our stories isn't about seeking validation or approval. Instead, it's about recognizing and owning our worth. It's about understanding that you are enough, just as you are, with all your imperfections and idiosyncrasies.

When we share our stories, we peel back layers of ourselves, revealing the authentic essence beneath. This vulnerability might seem daunting, but it's in this space that we can truly connect with others. Our shared experiences, feelings, and struggles create a common ground, a space for empathy and understanding to bloom.

In the process of sharing, we also embark on a journey of self-discovery. As we reflect on our experiences, we gain a deeper understanding of our strengths, our weaknesses, and the values that guide us. Our stories are not static; they evolve as we do, shaped by our experiences and the wisdom we garner along the way.

Sharing our narrative also opens the door for others to feel seen and heard. It's an opportunity to inspire, to encourage, and to remind others that they are not alone in their journeys. Your story could be the beacon of hope someone needs, the affirmation that they too, are enough.

However, it's important to approach the process of sharing your story with care. Be gentle with yourself, understanding that it's okay to choose which chapters you share and which ones you hold close. Remember that your story is your own, and you have the right to share it in your own time, in your own way.

In sharing your story, you might encounter skepticism or judgment. However, remember that your worth is not predicated on others' opinions. You are enough, irrespective of how your story is received. Your experiences, your feelings, your truths - they are valid and they matter.

As you move forward, hold onto the understanding that sharing your story is a gift - to yourself and to the world. It's an act of courage, a commitment to authenticity, and a testament to your resilience.

In the grand narrative of life, your story is a vital chapter. It's a piece of the universal puzzle, a slice of the collective human experience. So, take a deep breath, embrace your truth, and remember - you are enough. Your story matters. And in sharing it, you invite others to recognize their own worth, to embrace their own stories, and to understand that they too, are enough.

After all, our stories are more than mere recounts of our past. They are reflections of our journey, embodiments of our strength, and reminders of our inherent worth. They are the echoes of our existence, the footprints we leave behind. And in sharing them, we honor our journey and inspire others to do the same.

## Promoting Positivity

In our journey of self-discovery and self-acceptance, positivity plays an integral role. It is the beacon that illuminates our path, even in the darkest corners of our mind. It is the gentle nudge that encourages us to keep going, to persevere, and to believe that we are, indeed, enough.

Promoting positivity, however, does not mean denying the existence of negative emotions, nor does it mean forcing a smile when we feel like crying. It is not about painting a picture of perfection, but about finding the strength and resilience within us, amidst our imperfections. It is about acknowledging our feelings, understanding them, and then channeling them in a way that will lead us to a healthier mental and emotional state.

In our society, we are often bombarded with images and messages that suggest we are not enough. We are told that we need to be more, do more, and have more. These external pressures can lead us to internalize negativity, to question our worth, and to doubt our capabilities. To counteract these negative influences, we need to cultivate a positive mindset.

One of the key ways to promote positivity is through positive affirmations. These are statements that we make to ourselves, affirming our worth, our capabilities, and our potential. They can be as simple as "I am enough," "I am capable," or "I am deserving of love and respect." By repeating these affirmations regularly, we can start to replace the negative thoughts and beliefs that have taken root in our minds.

The power of positive affirmations lies in their ability to rewire our brains. When we repeat a statement often enough, our brain starts to accept it as truth. This is known as neuroplasticity, the ability of our brains to change and adapt. By harnessing this power, we can reshape our thoughts, our beliefs, and ultimately, our reality.

Another way to foster positivity is by practicing gratitude. Gratitude is a powerful tool that can shift our focus from what we lack to what we have. It reminds us of the good in our lives, helping us to appreciate our blessings, no matter how small they may seem. By acknowledging the good, we can cultivate a sense of contentment and fulfillment, reinforcing the belief that we are enough.

Lastly, we must remember to be kind to ourselves. Self-kindness is an essential part of promoting positivity. It means treating ourselves with the same compassion, understanding, and forgiveness that we would extend to others. It means allowing ourselves to make mistakes, to learn, and to grow. It means accepting ourselves as we are, recognizing that we are a work in progress, and that is perfectly okay.

Promoting positivity is a journey, not a destination. It is a process of unlearning negative beliefs, relearning positive ones, and continually reinforcing them. It requires patience, persistence, and above all, belief in ourselves. As we embark on this journey, let us remember that we are enough, just as we are. We are worthy, we are capable, and we are deserving of all the love, respect, and happiness that life has to offer.

## Empowering Others

In our journey towards self-discovery and self-acceptance, we often overlook a crucial aspect – the power of empowering others. Empowerment isn't just about gaining power for oneself; it's also about instilling that power in others. By helping others realize their worth and potential, we can foster a sense of community and shared growth that enriches our own lives as well.

In the context of this book, "You are Enough", empowerment begins with the understanding that each one of us, in our own unique way, is sufficient. To empower others, we must first embrace this truth for ourselves. It is only when we truly believe in our own worth, that we can genuinely inspire others to do the same.

Empowering others is not about making them dependent on us for their self-esteem or self-worth. Instead, it is about helping them unlock their inherent potential, helping them see that they, too, are enough. It is about creating a supportive environment where individuals can grow, learn, and build their self-confidence.

Empowerment doesn't demand grand gestures. Sometimes, it can be as simple as a kind word, a listening ear, or a shoulder to lean on. It's about acknowledging the strength in others, even when they can't see it themselves.

It's about validating their feelings, their struggles, and their victories. It's about standing by their side, cheering them on as they battle their demons and celebrate their achievements.

To empower others, we must learn to be empathetic. Empathy allows us to understand and share the feelings of another. It's the ability to step into someone else's shoes and view the world from their perspective. By empathizing with others, we can provide them with the emotional support and understanding they need to overcome their obstacles.

Empowerment is also about encouraging others to step out of their comfort zones. It's about pushing them to take risks, to strive for their dreams, and to never settle for less. It's about instilling in them the belief that they can achieve anything they set their mind to, that their dreams are valid, and that they are capable of realizing them.

However, empowering others does not mean imposing our beliefs, ideas or values on them. It is about providing them with the tools to make their own decisions, forge their own path, and define their own success. It is about respecting their individuality and appreciating their uniqueness.

When we empower others, we not only contribute to their personal growth but also to the betterment of our society. Empowered individuals are more likely to contribute positively to their communities, be it through leadership, innovation, or simply by being kinder, more compassionate human beings.

In essence, empowering others is a reflection of our own empowerment. When we are secure in our own worth, we feel no need to belittle others or hold them back. Instead, we uplift them, encourage them, and celebrate their successes as if they were our own.

As we continue on our journey towards self-acceptance and self-love, let us not forget the power of empowering others. For it is through empowering others that we truly realize our own strength, our own worth, and our own potential. Remember, empowerment is not a zero-sum game; the more we give, the more we grow.

# Chapter 7: Creating Impact

## Leading With Purpose

As I journeyed through the corridors of self-discovery, I found myself standing at the crossroads of purpose. The question that loomed large was, "What is my purpose?" The answer, I found, was not a destination but a journey. It was not a single, finite point, but an ever-evolving, dynamic process. It was not about being something, but about becoming. And at the heart of this becoming was leading with purpose.

Leading with purpose is a profound journey of self-realization. It is about aligning your actions with your core values and beliefs. It is about leading with authenticity, integrity, and compassion. It is about making a positive impact on the world around you.

To lead with purpose, one must first understand oneself. This understanding comes from introspection and self-reflection. It requires us to look deep within ourselves, to examine our values, our passions, our strengths, and our limitations. It requires us to confront our fears, our insecurities, our doubts. It is a journey that is often uncomfortable, but it is through this discomfort that we grow.

Leading with purpose is also about understanding others. It requires empathy and compassion. It requires us to listen, to understand, and to empathize with the experiences and perspectives of others. It requires us to recognize our shared humanity, to understand that we are all interconnected, that we are all part of a larger whole.

Leading with purpose is about making a difference. It is about using our talents, our skills, our resources to create positive change. It is about leaving a lasting legacy, about making the world a better place for future generations. It is about service, about giving back, about contributing to the well-being of others.

But leading with purpose is not without its challenges. It requires courage, resilience, and perseverance. It requires us to take risks, to step outside our comfort zones, to embrace uncertainty. It requires us to face failure, to learn from our mistakes, to rise again with renewed determination.

Yet, it is through these challenges that we find our strength. It is through these challenges that we discover our potential. It is through these challenges that we realize our purpose.

As I reflect on my own journey of leading with purpose, I am filled with gratitude. Gratitude for the lessons learned, for the growth experienced, for the impact made. It is a journey that has enriched my life, that has brought meaning and fulfillment, that has made me realize that I am enough.

Leading with purpose is not about being perfect. It is about being authentic. It is not about having all the answers. It is about asking the right questions. It is not about being in control. It is about letting go and trusting the process. It is not about achieving success. It is about finding fulfillment.

As we embark on our own journeys of leading with purpose, let us remember that we are enough. We are enough in our imperfections, in our struggles, in our victories. We are enough in our authenticity, in our vulnerability, in our courage. We are enough in our compassion, in our empathy, in our love. We are enough in our journey of becoming, in our journey of leading with purpose.

In the end, it is not about what we do, but who we become. And who we become is shaped by our purpose, by our values, by our actions. So, let us lead with purpose, with authenticity, with compassion. Let us lead with love, with courage, with resilience. Let us lead with the knowledge that we are enough.

## Fostering Community

As we journey through life, we often find ourselves in a constant struggle to be 'enough.' We yearn for acceptance, validation, and the comforting sense of belonging. In this vast universe, it is our human connection that anchors us, reminding us that we are not alone. It is the sense of community that helps us realize our self-worth and that indeed, we are enough.

A community is not merely a group of people living in the same place or sharing a common interest. It is a tapestry of individuals, each unique in their own way, yet woven together by the threads of shared values, mutual respect, and common goals. A community nurtures us, challenges us, and ultimately shapes us. It provides us with a platform to grow, learn, and contribute. It is within this context that we begin to understand that our worth is not determined by societal standards or external validation but is inherent within us.

Fostering such a nurturing community, however, is not a passive process. It requires effort, commitment, and a strong sense of empathy. It is about creating an environment where everyone feels safe to be themselves, to express their ideas, and to share their experiences. It is about encouraging open dialogues, promoting diversity, and celebrating individuality. It is about understanding that being 'enough' is not about being perfect but about being authentic.

Creating a community starts with us. We need to be the change we wish to see. We need to practice kindness, not just towards others, but towards ourselves as well. We need to acknowledge our strengths, embrace our flaws, and celebrate our uniqueness. We need to understand that our worth is not defined by our achievements, our failures, or our social status, but by who we are as individuals. We need to believe that we are enough just as we are.

Once we cultivate this mindset within ourselves, we can then extend it to others. We can create a community where everyone is valued for their individuality, where everyone is encouraged to express themselves freely, and where everyone is reminded that they are enough. We can foster a culture of acceptance and respect, a culture that celebrates diversity and promotes inclusivity.

In such a community, we not only find acceptance and validation, but we also find empowerment. We learn that our voices matter, that our ideas are valuable, and that our experiences are significant. We learn to appreciate our uniqueness and to celebrate our individuality. We learn to love ourselves for who we are, not for who we think we should be.

Fostering a community is not just about creating a safe space for individuals to be themselves. It is also about challenging individuals to be their best selves. It is about encouraging individuals to step out of their comfort zones, to embrace their flaws, and to strive for growth. It is about reminding individuals that they are enough, that they have always been enough, and that they will always be enough.

In the end, fostering a community is about creating a space where everyone feels seen, heard, and valued. It is about creating a space where everyone is reminded that they are enough, just as they are. It is about creating a space where everyone is encouraged to be their authentic selves, to embrace their uniqueness, and to strive for growth. It is about creating a space where everyone is reminded that they are not alone, that they are part of something bigger, and that they are part of a community.

## Making A Difference

In our journey of self-discovery, we often encounter a critical juncture, where we ask ourselves - how can I truly make a difference? How can I contribute my unique skills and talents in a way that positively impacts others and the world around me? These questions, while profound, are an integral part of understanding that indeed, you are enough.

When we contemplate on making a difference, it's important to remember that we are not required to scale mountains or part seas. Instead, real change often takes place in the smaller, quieter moments of life. It's in the kind words shared with a friend going through a tough time, the gentle hand that helps an elderly neighbour with their groceries, or the quiet dedication of a volunteer at a local shelter. In these moments, we realize that making a difference isn't necessarily about grand gestures, but about the consistent effort to make the world a little better each day.

Reflecting on our personal journey, it's essential to understand that we all possess unique gifts and talents. These are the tools that we have been given to make our mark on the world. Whether it's through our creativity, our compassion, our intelligence, or our resilience, we each have something valuable to contribute. Recognizing this is a crucial step towards making a difference.

However, it's also important to acknowledge that making a difference doesn't always mean being in the spotlight or receiving recognition. True change often happens behind the scenes, in the quiet moments when no one is watching. It's about making the conscious choice to do good, not for accolades or applause, but simply because it's the right thing to do.

Making a difference also requires courage. It involves stepping outside of our comfort zones and taking risks. It means standing up for what we believe in, even if it's unpopular. It's about being true to ourselves and our values, even when it's difficult. And most importantly, it's about understanding that we are enough, just as we are.

Remember, making a difference isn't about changing the world in one fell swoop, but about making a series of small changes that accumulate over time. It's about recognizing that we have the power to influence the world around us, in both big and small ways.

In the end, making a difference is about embracing our uniqueness and using it to positively impact others. It's about understanding that we are enough, just as we are. And it's about realizing that we are all connected, and that our actions, however small, can make a significant impact.

So, as you continue on your journey of self-discovery, remember this - you are enough, you have always been enough, and you will always be enough. You have the power to make a difference, in your own unique way. Embrace it, cherish it, and use it to make the world a better place.

## Contributing To Society

As we walk the path of self-awareness and self-acceptance, it becomes apparent that our journey doesn't end with us. Our existence is interconnected with the world around us, and as we learn to embrace our worth, we also discover the power we hold to make a difference. This realization marks our entry into the fourth subchapter, a space where we delve into the concept of contributing to society.

We are not solitary beings. We live in a society, in communities that thrive on cooperation and mutual support. As we grow and learn to acknowledge our worth, we also need to acknowledge our role within this larger structure. Contributing to society isn't just about giving back, it's about acknowledging our responsibility and fulfilling our role as part of a larger whole.

The first step towards this is to understand what we can offer. Each of us is unique, with our own set of skills, talents, and passions. These are not just tools for personal achievement, but also gifts that we can use to contribute to the world. Whether it's through our profession, our hobbies, or through volunteering, there are countless ways we can use our abilities for the benefit of others.

However, contributing to society isn't just about doing. It's also about being - being present, being empathetic, being understanding. It's about recognizing the humanity in others, and treating them with the dignity and respect they deserve. It's about standing up against injustice, and advocating for those who can't advocate for themselves. In essence, it's about embodying the values we wish to see in the world.

It's important to note that contributing to society doesn't require grand gestures or monumental efforts. Small acts of kindness, such as helping a neighbor, donating to a charity, or even just listening to someone who needs to be heard, can have a profound impact. It's not about the scale of the act, but the intent behind it.

As we contribute to society, we also contribute to ourselves. We gain a sense of purpose, a feeling of being connected to something larger than ourselves. We learn to see ourselves not just as individuals, but as integral parts of a community. We learn to value ourselves not just for who we are, but for the difference we can make.

But perhaps the most important lesson we learn is that we, as individuals, matter. Our actions matter. Our words matter. Our choices matter. And when we use them to contribute positively to society, we not only affirm our own worth, but also help others see their own.

So as we continue on our journey of self-discovery and self-acceptance, let's not forget the world around us. Let's not forget that we have the power to make a difference. Let's not forget that we are enough, not just for ourselves, but for the world. And let's use this knowledge to contribute to society, to make the world a little bit better, one act at a time. Because in the end, that's what being enough is all about.

# Leaving A Legacy

As we journey through the winding roads of life, we are often faced with the question: "What will we leave behind?" This is not simply a question of material possessions, but of the impact we have made on the world and on the lives of those we encounter. This is the essence of leaving a legacy.

The concept of legacy is often associated with grandeur, with monumental achievements that change the course of history. However, the true essence of a legacy is far more intimate, far more personal. It is the accumulation of our actions, our words, and our deeds that form the fabric of our legacy. It is the manner in which we have touched the lives of others, the difference we have made in their journey, that truly defines our legacy.

In the pursuit of leaving a legacy, we often overlook the most important element - ourselves. We are often so focused on the legacy we want to leave behind that we forget about the legacy we are living right now. Each day, each moment, is an opportunity to create a legacy that reflects our true selves, our values, and our passions. It is a chance to create a legacy that is a true reflection of who we are.

Leaving a legacy is not about achieving great things in the eyes of the world, but about making a difference in the lives of those around us. It is about living our lives in a way that inspires others, that encourages them to strive for their dreams, to believe in their potential, and to embrace their worth. It is about creating a ripple effect that extends far beyond our own lives, touching the lives of countless others in ways we may never fully understand.

Leaving a legacy is about living our truth, about being authentic in our thoughts, words, and actions. It is about being true to ourselves, to our values, and to our passions. It is about living a life that is congruent with who we truly are. This is the most powerful legacy we can leave behind - a legacy of authenticity, of integrity, and of love.

In the end, the most important legacy we can leave behind is that of love. Love is the most powerful force in the universe, capable of transforming lives and changing the course of history. It is the legacy of love that truly endures, that truly makes a difference.

So, as you journey through life, remember this: You are enough. You are enough just as you are, with all your flaws and imperfections, with all your strengths and weaknesses. You are enough to make a difference, to touch lives, to leave a legacy.

And so, dear reader, I leave you with this: Live your life with love, with authenticity, with passion. Live your life in a way that inspires others, that encourages them to embrace their worth, to believe in their potential. Live your life in a way that leaves a legacy of love, of authenticity, of integrity. For this is the most powerful legacy you can leave behind. This is your legacy. This is enough.

# Chapter 8: Embodying Mindfulness

## Being Present

In the world we live in today, our minds are often scattered, filled with worries about the future and regrets about the past. We are seldom truly present in the moment, and this lack of mindfulness can lead to a feeling of dissatisfaction and emptiness. It's as if we are always running, chasing after something that always seems just out of reach.

The world seems to be spinning faster and faster, and we are caught in the whirlwind, struggling to keep up with the pace. We are overwhelmed by the noise and distractions that surround us, and we often forget to listen to our own voices, our own hearts. We are so focused on doing, achieving, and acquiring that we forget to just be.

Being present means being fully engaged in the here and now, not lost in thoughts about the past or worries about the future. It means being aware of our surroundings, our thoughts, our feelings, and our bodies. It means accepting and embracing what is, without judgment or resistance.

Being present is not always easy, especially in a world that encourages us to be constantly on the go, always striving for more. But it is a practice, and like any other practice, it gets easier with time and consistency. It requires patience, compassion, and a willingness to slow down and pay attention.

The first step towards being present is to become aware of our own breath. When we focus on our breath, we bring our attention back to the present moment. We notice the sensation of the breath entering and leaving our bodies, the rise and fall of our chest, the feeling of the air on our skin. We become aware of the life force that sustains us, moment by moment.

Mindfulness is another key aspect of being present. Mindfulness is the practice of paying attention in a particular way: on purpose, in the present moment, and nonjudgmentally. It involves observing our thoughts and feelings without getting caught up in them. We notice them, acknowledge them, and let them pass by like clouds in the sky.

Being present also means being fully engaged in whatever we are doing. Whether we are washing dishes, walking in the park, or having a conversation with a friend, we bring our full attention to the task at hand. We immerse ourselves in the experience, savoring each moment as it unfolds.

When we are present, we are more in tune with ourselves and with the world around us. We become more aware of our own needs and the needs of others. We become more patient, more compassionate, more understanding. We become more resilient, more adaptable, more content.

Being present is not about escaping from the world, but rather about fully engaging with it. It's about appreciating the beauty of the ordinary, the magic of the mundane. It's about finding peace in the midst of chaos, joy in the midst of sorrow, love in the midst of fear.

In essence, being present is about realizing that we are enough, just as we are. We don't need to be more, do more, have more. We are enough, and in this moment, all is well.

## Practicing Gratitude

Life has an uncanny way of presenting us with challenges that can sometimes make us feel like we're not enough. We might find ourselves comparing our journey to that of others, questioning our worth, or feeling overwhelmed by the pressures of daily life. However, one powerful tool that can help us shift away from these negative thought patterns is the practice of gratitude.

Gratitude is often overlooked, seen as a mere formality rather than a transformative practice. But it's more than just saying thank you. It's about acknowledging the beauty of life in its entirety, the good and the bad. It's about recognizing that every experience, every moment, contributes to our journey of growth and self-discovery.

Practicing gratitude requires us to shift our perspective, to focus on the abundance rather than the lack. It's about seeing the glass as half full instead of half empty. This doesn't mean ignoring our problems or pretending everything is perfect. It means acknowledging our struggles, but also recognizing the lessons and growth that come from them. It's about finding the silver lining in every cloud, the rainbow after every storm.

Gratitude can be practiced in various ways. It can be as simple as taking a few moments each day to reflect on what we're grateful for. This could be anything from the roof over our heads to the love of our family and friends, or even the simple fact that we woke up to see another day. It could also involve expressing our gratitude to others, letting them know how much we appreciate them.

Another powerful way to practice gratitude is through journaling. Writing down what we're grateful for can help us become more aware of the good in our lives. It can also serve as a reminder of our blessings during tough times. Moreover, it can help us see patterns of positivity that we might have otherwise overlooked.

Practicing gratitude isn't always easy, especially during challenging times. It's easy to get caught up in our struggles and forget about the good things in our lives. But it's during these times that gratitude can be most powerful. It can help us stay grounded, remind us of our strengths, and give us hope.

When we practice gratitude, we're not only acknowledging the good in our lives but also affirming our worth. We're saying that we are enough, just as we are. We're saying that we don't need to be more, do more, or have more to be happy. We're saying that we have enough, we do enough, and most importantly, we are enough.

Through gratitude, we can learn to embrace ourselves, with all our strengths and weaknesses. We can learn to love and accept ourselves, just as we are. We can learn to see ourselves not as lacking, but as beings full of potential, full of worth.

In the end, practicing gratitude is about more than just being thankful. It's about embracing life in all its complexity, acknowledging our worth, and recognizing that we are, indeed, enough. So, let's start practicing gratitude, not just as a habit, but as a way of life. Because we are enough, just as we are.

## Cultivating Inner Peace

Often, we find ourselves caught in the whirlwind of external circumstances, constantly seeking validation, peace, and contentment from outside sources. But the key to true tranquility and fulfillment lies within us. The journey of self-discovery and self-improvement is an inward journey, a journey towards cultivating inner peace.

Inner peace is not a destination but a state of being. It is a conscious choice that we make every day, in every moment. It is about embracing our imperfections, our vulnerabilities, and owning our truth. It is about acknowledging our emotions without judgment, and letting them flow through us, rather than allowing them to define us.

Cultivating inner peace is about learning to quiet the noise of the external world and tuning into our inner voice. It is about learning to trust ourselves, to trust our intuition, our instincts, and our capabilities. It is about recognizing that we are not defined by our past or our circumstances, but by the choices we make in the present moment.

It is about learning to let go – of expectations, of control, of fear, of judgment. It is about accepting that while we cannot control everything that happens to us, we can control how we respond to it. It is about understanding that peace is not the absence of conflict, but the ability to cope with it.

Cultivating inner peace requires patience and practice. It involves mindfulness – being present in the moment, fully engaged in the here and now. It involves meditation – quieting the mind and focusing on the breath, allowing thoughts to come and go without judgment. It involves gratitude – acknowledging and appreciating the good in our lives, rather than focusing on what we lack.

It is about self-care – nurturing our mind, body, and spirit, and understanding that we cannot serve others from an empty vessel. It is about setting boundaries and learning to say no, recognizing that we are not responsible for other people's happiness, and that it is okay to put ourselves first.

Cultivating inner peace is about self-acceptance – embracing who we are, as we are, and understanding that we are enough. It is about letting go of the need for validation from others, and finding validation within ourselves. It is about understanding that our worth is not determined by our achievements, our possessions, or our status, but by the love and kindness we show to ourselves and others.

Cultivating inner peace is about finding balance – balancing our personal and professional lives, our needs and wants, our dreams and reality. It is about understanding that life is a journey, not a race, and that every step we take on this journey is a step towards growth and evolution.

Cultivating inner peace is about understanding that we are not alone in our struggles, that we are all connected, and that we are all part of something greater than ourselves. It is about recognizing that we are all human, that we all make mistakes, and that it is through these mistakes that we learn and grow.

Cultivating inner peace is a journey, not a destination. It is a journey of self-discovery, self-improvement, and self-love. It is a journey towards understanding that we are enough, just as we are.

## Balancing Work and Play

As we navigate through the journey of life, we often find ourselves entangled in the web of responsibilities, commitments, and work. We tend to prioritize our professional life, forgetting to pause, breathe, and bask in the joy of living. The essence of life, however, lies in striking a balance - a balance between work and play, duty and leisure, commitment and relaxation.

We are often told that success is synonymous with hard work, with no room for leisure and relaxation. Yet, it is crucial to understand that the human spirit thrives not just on achievements and accomplishments but also on joy, laughter, and play. The rhythm of life is not just about the hustle and bustle of work but also about the stillness and peace found in moments of relaxation.

Our worth is not solely defined by our productivity. We are more than our jobs, our roles, and our responsibilities. We are human beings with a capacity for joy, creativity, and play. We deserve to take breaks, to rest, to engage in activities that bring us joy and happiness. We need to remind ourselves that it is okay to prioritize our well-being and happiness over our work.

The notion of balance is not about dividing our time equally between work and play but about integrating both aspects into our lives harmoniously. It is about recognizing when to push ourselves and when to step back and rest. It is about understanding that our worth is not dependent on our productivity but on our inherent humanity.

In the pursuit of balance, it is essential to set boundaries. We need to assert our right to time for relaxation and play without feeling guilty or unproductive. We need to understand that it is okay to say no to additional responsibilities if they infringe upon our personal time. We need to respect our need for downtime and ensure that we allocate time for activities that bring us joy and rejuvenation.

It is also important to cultivate a mindset of mindfulness and presence. Instead of constantly worrying about the future or dwelling on the past, we should strive to live in the present moment, savoring each experience as it comes. This mindset allows us to fully engage in our work when it is time to work and fully enjoy our leisure time when it is time to play.

In our quest for balance, we may sometimes stumble and falter. There may be periods when work takes precedence, and there may be times when we need to prioritize our leisure. This is all part of the process, and it is okay. The key is to continuously strive for balance, to make adjustments as needed, and to be kind to ourselves along the way.

Remember, you are enough. You are enough with your achievements and your failures, with your work and your play, with your strengths and your weaknesses. You are enough just as you are, in all your complexity and simplicity, in all your seriousness and playfulness.

Balancing work and play is not just about productivity and relaxation. It is about honoring our human need for both activity and rest, for both achievement and enjoyment. It is about acknowledging that we are multi-dimensional beings, capable of both hard work and deep play. It is about embracing our wholeness and celebrating our inherent worth. This leads to new experiences that we have and also helps to bring mind and body in coherence.

So, let us strive to balance work and play, not because we need to prove our worth, but because we recognize that we are enough, just as we are. Let us remember that the essence of life lies not just in doing, but also in being, not just in working, but also in playing. Let us embrace the rhythm of life, with all its ups and downs, its hustle and its peace, its work and its play.

## Living Intentionally

In the grand mosaic of life, we often find ourselves being pulled in multiple directions, swayed by external forces, societal norms, or cultural expectations. It is easy to lose sight of our true selves in this whirlwind of influences. However, the essence of our being, our true worth, lies not in these external factors but within us. This realization is the first step towards living intentionally, and it is a journey that requires courage, introspection, and a strong sense of self.

Living intentionally means making conscious choices about every aspect of our lives, from the mundane to the profound. It is about making decisions that align with our core values and beliefs, rather than simply going along with the flow or succumbing to societal pressures. It is about recognizing that we are the authors of our own lives and that every decision we make is a brushstroke on the canvas of our existence.

To live intentionally, we must first understand who we are at our core. This self-awareness is not about the roles we play – as a parent, a partner, an employee, or a friend – but about our essence, our values, our passions, and our dreams. It is about peeling back the layers of societal expectations and self-imposed limitations to reveal our true selves.

Once we have a clear understanding of who we are, we can begin to make decisions that align with our true selves. This might mean choosing a career that fulfills us rather than one that merely pays the bills, or it might mean prioritizing personal growth over material possessions. It might mean choosing to spend our time with people who uplift us rather than those who drain us, or it might mean setting boundaries to protect our mental and emotional health.

Living intentionally also means being present in each moment. It means being fully engaged in whatever we are doing, whether it's washing the dishes, spending time with loved ones, or working on a project. It means appreciating the beauty in the mundane and finding joy in the ordinary. It means being mindful of our thoughts, feelings, and actions, and recognizing that each moment is a gift to be cherished.

However, living intentionally is not always easy. It requires courage to go against the grain, to make decisions that might not be popular or understood by others. It requires discipline to stay true to our values and beliefs, even when it's tempting to compromise. It requires resilience to weather the storms of life and to keep moving forward, even when the path is unclear.

But despite these challenges, living intentionally is worth it. It allows us to live a life that is authentic and fulfilling, rather than one that is dictated by external forces. It allows us to be true to ourselves, to honor our worth, and to live in alignment with our true nature. It allows us to say, with conviction and without hesitation, "I am enough."

So, let us embark on this journey of intentional living, embracing the beauty of our individuality, and honoring the truth of our worth. Let us remember that we are not defined by the roles we play or the expectations of others, but by who we are at our core. Let us live intentionally, not just for ourselves, but for the world that needs our unique gifts and talents. After all, we are enough, just as we are.

# Chapter 9: Maintaining Balance

## Managing Stress

Reflecting on my own experiences, I've come to understand that stress is an inevitable part of life. It's a universal human experience, an unavoidable reality that we all must contend with. But it's also a personal journey that each of us navigates in our own unique way. How we manage stress can significantly influence our physical health, mental well-being, and overall quality of life.

In the fast-paced, high-pressure world we live in, stress is often viewed as a negative force. We're told to avoid it at all costs, to strive for a stress-free existence. But the truth is, stress isn't inherently bad. In fact, it's a natural response to challenging or demanding situations. It's our body's way of preparing us to face these challenges, to push through adversity and come out stronger on the other side. It is just that we don't know how to handle it.

The key, I've found, is not to eliminate stress entirely, but to manage it effectively. To learn how to harness its energy and use it as a tool for growth and self-improvement. To recognize when it's getting out of control and take steps to bring it back into balance.

One of the most powerful ways to manage stress is through self-care. This can take many forms, from physical activities like exercise and yoga, to mental practices like meditation and mindfulness. It's about taking time for yourself, prioritizing your needs, and nurturing your body and mind.

Another crucial aspect of stress management is maintaining a positive mindset. It can be tempting to get caught up in negative thoughts, especially when we're feeling overwhelmed. Negative thinking can quickly spiral out of control and lead to various mental health challenges. However, by choosing to concentrate on the good things in our lives and embracing gratitude, we have the power to change our outlook and lessen the effects of stress.

It's also important to remember that it's okay to ask for help. We often feel like we have to handle everything on our own, but that's simply not the case. Whether it's reaching out to a friend or family member, seeking professional help, or joining a support group, there are many resources available to help us cope with stress.

In my own journey, I've learned that managing stress is not about striving for perfection or avoiding challenges. It's about embracing our imperfections, confronting our fears, and learning to navigate the ups and downs of life with grace and resilience.

I've also realized that managing stress is a lifelong journey. It's not something that can be achieved overnight. It requires patience, perseverance, and a willingness to continually learn and grow. But the rewards are well worth the effort. By learning to manage stress effectively, we can improve our health, enhance our well-being, and live more fulfilling lives.

In the end, managing stress is about acknowledging that we are enough. That we have the strength and resilience to overcome any challenges that comes our way. That we are capable of creating a balanced, fulfilling life, regardless of the stressors we face.

So, take a deep breath, embrace your journey, and remember: you are enough.

## Promoting Wellness

As we journey through life, we often stumble upon obstacles that challenge our sense of self-worth and well-being. Sometimes, we might even find ourselves questioning whether we are enough. However, it is important to remember that wellness is not a destination, but a continuous journey. It is a journey that requires us to be proactive, nurturing, and forgiving towards ourselves. And this journey begins with the understanding that we are, indeed, enough.

Wellness is not just about being physically fit. It is a holistic concept that encompasses physical, mental, emotional, and spiritual health. It is about achieving a balance in all aspects of our lives and maintaining a state of optimal well-being. This means taking care of our bodies by eating a balanced diet, getting regular exercise, and getting enough sleep. It also means taking care of our minds by engaging in activities that stimulate our intellect and creativity, and our emotional well-being by maintaining healthy relationships and expressing our feelings in a constructive manner.

However, promoting wellness is not always easy. It requires commitment, discipline, and sometimes, making tough decisions. It might mean choosing to eat a salad instead of a burger, taking a walk instead of watching TV, or choosing to confront a difficult situation instead of avoiding it. But remember, every small step you take towards wellness counts. It is not about perfection, but progress.

One of the key aspects of promoting wellness is self-care. Self-care is not selfish. It is about recognizing our needs and taking the time to meet them. It is about setting boundaries and saying no when necessary. It is about taking care of ourselves so we can take care of others. After all, you cannot pour from an empty cup.

Self-care can take many forms. It could be as simple as taking a few minutes each day to meditate or journal, or it could involve taking a vacation to recharge. The important thing is to find what works for you and make it a part of your routine. The more you practice self-care, the more you will realize that you are enough.

Another key aspect of promoting wellness is cultivating a positive mindset. Often, we are our own worst critics. We are quick to judge ourselves and slow to forgive. However, it is important to remember that we are all works in progress. We all make mistakes and have flaws. But these do not define us. What defines us is our ability to learn from our mistakes and grow. So, instead of beating yourself up over a mistake, acknowledge it, learn from it, and move on. Cultivate a mindset of growth and resilience.

Promoting wellness also means seeking help when necessary. It is okay when you are not happy or feeling a bit left out. We all have moments of weakness, moments when we feel overwhelmed. During these times, do not hesitate to seek help. Reach out to a trusted friend, a family member, or a professional. Remember, seeking help is not a sign of weakness, but a sign of strength. It shows that you really care for your well being. But be careful about whom you seek help from. It is crucial to avoid seeking out individuals with low emotional intelligence. Engaging in conversations with such individuals may result in them solely sharing their own experiences and perspectives. This could potentially lead to the emergence of further complications.

Promoting wellness is an incredible expedition of self-discovery, self-care, and personal development. It entails acknowledging and accepting our intrinsic worthiness. By actively tending to our physical, mental, and spiritual well-being, we can foster a constructive outlook on life. Start this incredible journey towards wellness and always remember, you possess everything you need.

## Finding Harmony

In the labyrinth of life, we often find ourselves lost, unsure of our true purpose or direction. Amidst the cacophony of societal expectations, personal desires, and inherent insecurities, the melody of our authentic selves gets drowned out. It is in these moments of disarray that we must seek harmony, not in the external world, but within ourselves.

Harmony, in its purest form, is an alignment of elements that creates a beautiful balance. In the context of our lives, it refers to the equilibrium between our thoughts, words, actions, and emotions. It is about accepting our past, being present in our current moment, and having faith in our future. But, how does one find this elusive harmony?

Finding harmony starts with self-acceptance. It is about acknowledging our strengths and weaknesses, our triumphs, and failures. Our essence is a collection of everything we have been through, felt, and done. Embracing this truth doesn't mean giving up or being content with where we are; it means recognizing our present situation and using it as a springboard for growth. It's all about showing ourselves the same empathy and care that we show to those around us.

Once we accept ourselves, we can start to understand our values and priorities better. Harmony is not about having a perfect life, but about aligning our lives with what truly matters to us. It is about living authentically, in accordance with our core beliefs and values. This requires introspection and honesty, to look within and identify what truly matters to us.

Finding harmony also means letting go of the things that hold us back. It means recognizing and releasing the fears, insecurities, and past hurts that keep us stuck in a cycle of self-doubt and self-criticism. It's about understanding that our worth is not defined by external factors, but by our own perception of ourselves. It's about forgiving ourselves and others, releasing the weight of resentment and regret that we've been carrying around. It is imperative that we embrace the responsibility of owning our thoughts, words, and actions.

Finding harmony is not a one-time endeavor, but a continuous journey. It requires patience, perseverance, and a willingness to be vulnerable. It's about continually reassessing our lives, adjusting our course when necessary, and being open to growth and change. It's about striving for balance, not perfection.

In this quest for harmony, it's essential to remember that we are enough. We are enough in our victories and in our defeats, in our joys and in our sorrows. We are enough in our solitude and in our relationships, in our aspirations and in our achievements. We are enough, not because of what we do or have, but because of who we are.

Finding harmony is about finding ourselves, about embracing our uniqueness and individuality. It's about celebrating our journey, with all its twists and turns, highs and lows. It's about finding peace within ourselves, amidst the chaos of the world around us. It's about understanding that we are enough, just as we are. Because, in the end, harmony is not something we find; it's something we create.

## Prioritizing Self

Often, we find ourselves trapped in the whirlwind of trying to meet everyone else's needs before our own. We run ourselves ragged trying to be everything for everyone - the perfect parent, the loyal friend, the dedicated employee - often at the expense of our own health and happiness. We push our own needs to the backburner, telling ourselves we'll find time for them later, but later never seems to come. It's a cycle that repeats itself, leaving us depleted and unfulfilled.

It is vital for us to admit the indisputable truth that we cannot offer help when our resources are drained. We cannot effectively serve others if we are running on empty ourselves. This is where the concept of prioritizing self comes into play. Self-prioritization is not about being selfish or neglecting our responsibilities. Rather, it is about recognizing the importance of maintaining our own physical, emotional, and mental health so that we can be our best selves for the people we care about.

Prioritizing self is about setting boundaries and allowing ourselves to say "no" when we need to. It's about understanding that it's okay to not be available for everyone, all the time. It's about taking time for self-care, whether that means taking a relaxing bath, reading a good book, or simply spending time in solitude. It's about nurturing our own interests and passions, and not feeling guilty for doing so.

It's common to think that focusing on ourselves is self-centered, but it's important to realize that self-care is not only a treat, but a requirement. It's a key part of leading a harmonious and satisfying life. When we neglect our own needs, we risk burning out, which can affect our ability to care for others and perform our responsibilities.

Moreover, when we prioritize ourselves, we teach others how to treat us. We show them that we value ourselves and our time, and that we expect them to do the same. This not only improves our own self-esteem but also fosters healthier relationships with others. After all, respect and understanding are two-way streets.

Prioritizing self also means taking responsibility for our own happiness. It's about understanding that we are in control of our own lives, and that it's up to us to create the life we want. It's about not relying on others for our happiness, but finding it within ourselves.

It's important to remember that prioritizing self is about constantly reassessing our needs and making adjustments as necessary. It's about learning to listen to our inner voice and trusting our instincts.

In conclusion, prioritizing self is about recognizing our worth and treating ourselves with the love and respect we deserve. It's about finding the courage to put ourselves first, not out of selfishness, but out of a deep understanding of our own worth and value. So, take a step back, breathe, and remember: you are enough. You always have been, and you always will be. Prioritize yourself, because you are worth it.

## Embracing Rest

As we journey through the landscape of personal growth and self-acceptance, it's easy to find ourselves ensnared in the trap of constant striving. We are often conditioned to believe that rest is a luxury, a reward we must earn through hard work, achievement, and perpetual motion. We hustle, we grind, we push, all in the pursuit of this elusive state of 'enoughness.' But what if we paused for a moment and reimagine rest not as a reward, but as a fundamental necessity?

Rest is not a sign of weakness, nor is it an indication of laziness. It is a vital part of our well-being and a crucial component of self-love. When we allow ourselves to rest, we are not only replenishing our physical energy but also nurturing our emotional and mental health. We're giving ourselves permission to recharge, to refresh, and to renew our spirit.

Rest is a form of self-respect. It's an acknowledgment that we are not invincible machines, but human beings with limits and needs. By embracing rest, we are saying to ourselves, "I am worth taking care of. I am worth the time it takes to rejuvenate. I am enough just as I am, without having to prove anything or achieve everything."

But how do we embrace rest in a world that glorifies busyness and productivity? We start by changing our perspective. We need to stop viewing rest as an optional extra and start seeing it as a vital part of our holistic health. We need to recognize that rest is not just about sleeping or lounging on the couch – it's about creating space in our lives for quiet reflection, for mindfulness, for simply being in the present moment.

Embracing rest also means setting boundaries. It means saying no to things that drain us and yes to things that nourish us. It means prioritizing our well-being over societal expectations or external pressures. Taking care of ourselves is crucial, as it teaches us the valuable lesson that we can't give what we don't have. It's not about being selfish, but rather recognizing the necessity of self-care. Health experts recommend a good 6-8 hours of sleep per night for a healthy individual. However, it's important to be mindful that exceeding 8 hours might lead to an unhealthy habit, potentially compromising our overall well-being.

Rest is not just about physical relaxation, but also about mental and emotional rejuvenation. It allows us to recharge our batteries, clear our minds, and reconnect with ourselves on a deeper level. In a world that glorifies busyness and productivity, taking time to rest can feel like a radical act of rebellion against societal norms that equate worth with constant activity.

By embracing rest, we are acknowledging our own humanity and limitations. We are recognizing that we are not machines that can operate at full capacity 24/7. Rest is a necessary component of a healthy and balanced life, and neglecting it can lead to burnout, stress, and a host of other physical and mental health issues.

In a culture that often values productivity over well-being, prioritizing rest can be a revolutionary act of self-love and self-care. It is a way of honoring our bodies, minds, and spirits, and recognizing that we deserve time to simply be, without the pressure to constantly achieve and excel.

Let us challenge the notion that rest is a sign of weakness or laziness and embrace rest. Let's give ourselves permission to slow down, to recharge, to just be. Let's honor our need for downtime, for quiet, for reflection. Let's remember that we are not machines, but beautifully complex human beings who need rest to thrive.

# Chapter 10: Strengthening Resilience

## Facing Fears

As we navigate the intricate maze of existence, we are bound to come face to face with the elusive apparitions of apprehension that hide in its recesses. These are the hidden adversaries that we wrestle with, frequently disguised as uncertainty, self-doubt, and the persistent notion of inadequacy. It is in these moments that we must face our fears, stand tall, and remember that we are, indeed, enough.

Fear is a formidable opponent. It is an insidious force that can creep into our minds, paralyzing us from taking action, from pursuing our dreams, and from living a life that is authentically ours. It whispers in our ears that we are inadequate, incapable, and unworthy. Yet, these are nothing more than illusions - mere constructions of our minds.

Facing our fears is not a battle to be won in a single day. It requires courage, resilience, and a steadfast belief in our own worthiness. We must be willing to look deeply within ourselves, to confront the shadows that lurk within and to challenge the narratives that we have constructed about who we are and what we are capable of.

What is Fear? Fear is a complex emotion tied to our ability to predict the future. It often leads us to focus on the worst-case scenario, limiting our potential and hindering personal growth. However, by shifting our mindset to positivity, we can approach situations with optimism and hope. This empowers us to be resilient, adaptable, and open-minded, leading to personal development and success. Embracing a positive mindset not only benefits us individually but also inspires and uplifts those around us. By focusing on positive outcomes, we become a beacon of hope for others struggling with their own fears. That can help us to deal with fear. Other form of fear is self doubt.

In this process, we must cultivate a sense of self-compassion. Yet, it is in these moments of self-doubt that we need to extend kindness and understanding towards ourselves and others. We need to remember that we are human, that we are fallible, and that it is okay to make mistakes. It is through these mistakes that we learn, grow, and become stronger.

It is also important to remember that fear is not inherently negative. It serves as a protective mechanism, warning us of potential dangers and risks. However, when fear becomes pervasive, when it holds us back from pursuing our dreams and living our truth, it becomes a barrier that we need to overcome.

Facing our fears also involves embracing vulnerability. It requires us to let go of the need to appear perfect, to meet the expectations of others, and to fit into society's molds. It is about acknowledging our fears, accepting our imperfections, and celebrating our unique selves.

As we navigate through this journey of facing our fears, we will undoubtedly stumble and fall. Yet, it is in these moments of struggle that we truly discover our strength and resilience. We realize that we are much more than our fears, that we are capable of overcoming adversity, and that we are indeed enough.

Remember, you are enough just as you are. You do not need to be more, do more, or have more to be worthy. Your worthiness is inherent. It does not depend on external validation or achievements. It is rooted in your very existence, in your humanity, and in your capacity for love, compassion, and kindness.

So, face your fears. Embrace your vulnerability. Celebrity your uniqueness. And never forget that you are enough. You always have been, and you always will be.

## Overcoming Obstacles

As we traverse the winding road of life, we inevitably encounter obstacles. These hurdles, whether they be physical, emotional, or mental, often seem insurmountable. They tower over us, casting long, daunting shadows that obscure our path forward. Yet, it is crucial to remember that these obstacles are not the end of our journey, but rather an integral part of it.

Every obstacle we face is a stepping stone on our path to personal growth. In the face of adversity, we often discover hidden reserves of strength and resilience within ourselves that we never knew existed. It is through overcoming these challenges that we grow stronger, wiser, and more capable. The struggle, though painful, is a necessary part of our growth process.

However, it is not enough to simply overcome obstacles. We must also learn from them. Each hurdle we face is a lesson waiting to be learned. It is an opportunity for reflection, introspection, and growth. By taking the time to understand the challenges we face, we can gain valuable insights about ourselves and the world around us.

Remember, you are enough. You possess within you all the strength and courage you need to overcome any obstacle that stands in your way. You need not seek validation or approval from others. Your worth is inherent, and it is not defined by the challenges you face, but by how you choose to face them.

Yet, it is also important to remember that it's okay to ask for help. We are not meant to face these challenges alone. Reaching out to others in times of struggle is not a sign of weakness, but of strength. It shows that you have the courage to admit your struggles and seek the support you need.

Overcoming obstacles is not about proving your worth to others. It is about proving it to yourself. It is about learning to trust in your own strength and resilience. It is about realizing that you are capable of more than you ever thought possible.

Remember, every obstacle you face is an opportunity. An opportunity to grow, to learn, and to become a stronger, more resilient version of yourself. So, the next time you find yourself facing a seemingly insurmountable hurdle, take a moment to reflect. What can this challenge teach you? How can it help you grow?

In the face of adversity, remember to be kind to yourself. It's okay to stumble. It's okay to fall. What matters is that you pick yourself up, dust yourself off, and keep moving forward.

Never forget, you are enough. You have within you all the strength, courage, and resilience you need to conquer any obstacle that life throws your way. So, face those challenges with confidence, knowing that you are more than capable of overcoming them.

In conclusion, obstacles are not roadblocks on our path, but stepping stones. They are opportunities for growth and self-discovery. So, embrace them. Learn from them. Grow from them. And always remember - you are enough.

## Building Mental Toughness

Throughout our journey in life, we are often tested in ways that push us beyond our comfort zones. These moments of challenge and adversity are not mere obstacles, but opportunities for growth. They allow us to build and strengthen our mental toughness, a quality that is imperative to our well-being and success. And it is in these moments that we need to remind ourselves that we are enough.

Mental toughness is not about being invincible or immune to pain and struggle. It is about acknowledging our feelings, accepting our flaws, and still choosing to move forward. It is the resilience to rise after every fall, the courage to face our fears, and the conviction to persist in the face of adversity. It is about embracing our vulnerabilities and transforming them into strengths.

Building mental toughness is a process. It doesn't happen overnight. It requires consistent effort, patience, and a willingness to step out of our comfort zones. It's about pushing our boundaries, challenging our limits, and daring to venture into the unknown. It's about embracing the discomfort, for it is in the midst of struggle that we find our strength.

The first step in building mental toughness is to change our mindset. We need to shift from a mindset of scarcity, where we constantly feel that we are lacking, to one of abundance, where we recognize and appreciate what we have. We need to stop comparing ourselves to others and start appreciating our unique journey. We need to understand that it's okay to make mistakes and fail. It's okay to not have all the answers. It's okay to be imperfect. Because we are enough.

The second step involves cultivating self-compassion. Frequently, we tend to be excessively critical of ourselves. We chastise ourselves for our imperfections and fixate on our disappointments. However, this approach only diminishes our self-assurance and obstructs our personal development. Instead, it is imperative that we extend kindness and empathy towards ourselves. We must recognize our endeavors, commemorate even the slightest triumphs, and grant ourselves forgiveness for our errors. For we possess inherent worth and sufficiency.

The third step is to nourish a positive attitude. Life will always have its ups and downs. But how we perceive these experiences determines how we are affected by them. We can choose to view challenges as insurmountable obstacles or as opportunities for growth. We can choose to dwell on the negative or focus on the positive. By cultivating a positive attitude, we empower ourselves to navigate life's ups and downs with grace and resilience.

Finally, building mental toughness involves taking care of our physical health. Our mind and body are interconnected, and neglecting one can adversely affect the other. Regular exercise, a balanced diet, adequate sleep - these are all crucial for our mental well-being. By taking care of our physical health, we fortify our mental strength.

## Harnessing Hope

In the vast ocean of life, hope serves as our beacon of light, guiding us through the darkest storms and the most violent waves. It is in this chapter that we delve into the transformative power of hope and how it can be help to foster personal growth.

For many, hope seems like a fleeting, ephemeral concept, a mere wish or desire that things will get better. It is often perceived as passive, something that happens to us rather than something we actively cultivate. However, in reality, hope is an active, dynamic force that can be harnessed and directed towards positive change. It is not just a fleeting feeling, but a mindset, a perspective, a way of life.

In our journey towards self-acceptance and self-love, hope plays a crucial role. It is the fuel that keeps us going when the road gets tough, the light that illuminates our path when everything else seems dark. Hope is not just about expecting the best, but also about being prepared for the worst. It is about having the courage to face our fears, our doubts, our insecurities, and still choosing to move forward.

Harnessing hope begins with recognizing its power. It is about understanding that hope is not just a wishful thought, but a powerful tool that can be used to overcome challenges and create positive change. It is about believing in our capacity to grow, to learn, to overcome, to become the best versions of ourselves. It involves embracing the potential for a brighter future, regardless of how bleak the current circumstances may appear.

But how do we remain hopeful? The first step is to cultivate a hopeful mindset. This means focusing on the positive, looking for the silver lining in every situation, and believing in our capacity to overcome. It means bouncing back from setbacks, and never giving up, no matter how difficult things get.

The second step is to set realistic, achievable goals. Hope is not about wishful thinking, but about setting clear, concrete goals that we can work towards. It is about breaking down our dreams into manageable steps and celebrating our progress along the way.

The third step is to surround ourselves with positivity. This means surrounding ourselves with people who believe in us, who inspire us, who lift us up. It means filling our minds with positive thoughts, our hearts with positive feelings, and our lives with positive experiences.

The fourth step is to practice gratitude. Gratitude is a powerful tool that can shift our focus from what's wrong in our lives to what's right. It can help us appreciate the good in our lives, cultivate positivity, and foster hope.

In conclusion, hope is not just an emotion, but a powerful force that can be harnessed for personal growth and resilience. So, let's harness hope, let's embrace its power, let's allow it to guide us towards a brighter, happier, more fulfilling future. For, in the words of Desmond Tutu, "Hope is being able to see that there is light despite all of the darkness." And remember, you are enough to change your future.

## Persevering Through Challenges

In the journey of life, we often encounter obstacles that seem insurmountable. These challenges may appear in various forms; personal loss, professional setbacks, health crises, or emotional struggles, to name a few. Regardless of their nature, they tend to shake our faith, disrupt our peace, and test our resilience. However, it is crucial to remember that these trials are not meant to break us, but to shape us, to help us grow and discover our true potential.

One of the most remarkable aspects of human nature is our ability to persevere, to endure hardships and still hold on to hope. This ability to press on, even when the odds are against us, is what defines our character and determines our destiny. It's not about how many times we fall, but how many times we get back up, dust ourselves off, and continue on our path with renewed determination.

Every challenge we face is an opportunity to learn, to grow, and to become stronger. When we face adversity, we are forced to confront our fears, our insecurities, and our self-doubts. We are compelled to question our beliefs, our values, and our self-worth. This process can be incredibly painful and disorienting. However, it is through this process of self-examination and self-discovery that we begin to understand who we truly are and what we are truly capable of.

Our struggles do not define us, but our response to them does. It is easy to feel overwhelmed and defeated when we are faced with adversity. It is easy to lose hope and give up. But it is in these moments of despair that we must dig deep within ourselves and find the strength to persevere.

Perseverance is not about being fearless or invincible. It is about having the courage to face our fears, the resilience to bounce back from setbacks, and the determination to keep going, no matter what. It is about recognizing that we are enough, just as we are, with all our flaws and imperfections.

It is important to remember that we are not alone in our struggles. We all face challenges, big and small, at different points in our lives. We all experience moments of self-doubt, fear, and uncertainty. But it is through these shared experiences of struggle and perseverance that we find connection, understanding, and empathy.

In the end, it is not the challenges we face that define us, but how we choose to respond to them. Do we choose to let them defeat us, or do we choose to rise above them? Do we choose to dwell on our failures, or do we choose to learn from them and move forward? Do we choose to let our fears hold us back, or do we choose to face them head-on and push through?

Persevering through difficulties entails more than mere survival; it involves flourishing. It requires discovering the resilience within ourselves to persist, regardless of the arduousness of the path. It necessitates acknowledging our inherent worth and realizing that we possess the capability to conquer any hurdles that life presents us.

So, remember, when you are faced with a challenge, don't see it as a roadblock, but as a stepping stone. Don't see it as a setback, but as a setup for a comeback. Don't see it as a sign that you are not enough, but as a reminder that you are more than enough. And most importantly, don't give up. Keep persevering, keep pushing, and keep believing in yourself. Because you are enough, and you always have been.

# Chapter 11: Unlocking Creativity

## Igniting Imagination

As we navigate the intricate maze of life, we frequently encounter moments of doubt regarding our value and adequacy. This self-doubt, this nagging insecurity, often stems from the societal norms and expectations that we are conditioned to conform to. However, it's time to let go of these inhibitions, these self-imposed limitations, and embrace the simple yet profound truth that we are enough, just as we are.

The first step towards embodying this truth is to ignite our imagination. Imagination is a powerful tool, it's the canvas on which we paint our dreams and aspirations. It's the blueprint of our desired reality. It's the wellspring from which our most creative ideas, our most innovative solutions, and our most transformative changes emerge. When we nurture and ignite our imagination, we unlock the potential to become the architects of our own lives, the authors of our own stories.

Yet, so often, we let our imagination lay dormant, stifled by the fear of judgment, the fear of failure, the fear of stepping out of our comfort zones. We let the voices of doubt and criticism, both internal and external, overshadow the whispers of our dreams. We let the practicalities and pressures of the 'real world' extinguish the flame of our imagination. But it's time to reignite that flame, to let it burn brightly and illuminate our path forward.

Igniting our imagination starts with giving ourselves the permission to dream, to explore, to experiment, to make mistakes, and most importantly, to be our authentic selves. It's about embracing the unknown, embracing the uncertainty, and embracing the endless possibilities that life offers. It's about seeing challenges as opportunities for growth, seeing failures as stepping stones to success, seeing obstacles as detours in the right direction.

When we ignite our imagination, we give ourselves the freedom to envision a life where we are not confined by the shackles of societal norms, but are free to forge our own path, follow our own passions, and fulfill our own purpose. We give ourselves the freedom to envision a life where we are not striving to meet the expectations of others, but are striving to meet our own expectations, striving to become the best version of ourselves.

Imagination is not just about conjuring up images of what could be, it's about believing in the possibility of what could be. It's about having the courage to turn those possibilities into realities. It's about realizing that we are not just passive participants in life, but active creators of our life.

So, let's ignite our imagination. Let's dream big, let's think outside the box, let's push the boundaries of what's possible. Let's not just imagine a life where we are enough, let's live a life where we know that every day we are exploring our life. Because when we ignite our imagination, we ignite our potential, we ignite our power, we ignite our purpose. And most importantly, we ignite our belief in ourselves, our belief in our worth, our belief in our enough-ness.

Your dreams, your desires, your aspirations are enough. Your successes, your failures, your struggles, your triumphs are enough. You, in all your complexity and simplicity, in all your perfection and imperfection, in all your strength and vulnerability, are enough. So, ignite your imagination, and create a life that is a true reflection of you.

## Embracing Innovation

The journey of self-discovery and self-acceptance is often characterized by a myriad of experiences, emotions, and ideas. One of the most profound aspects of this journey is the realization that we are not static beings. We are constantly evolving, growing, and learning. This realization is what leads us to the concept of embracing innovation.

Innovation, by its very definition, is the process of introducing new ideas, methods, or devices. It is the heart of progress and growth. However, when we talk about innovation in the context of personal growth, it goes beyond just technological or scientific advancements. It refers to the endless potential within ourselves to create, transform, and evolve.

At first glance, it might seem counterintuitive. So, how does the concept of innovation fit into this?

The answer lies in understanding that being enough does not mean being static or stagnant. It means recognizing and accepting our current state while also acknowledging our potential for growth and transformation. Embracing innovation is about realizing that while we are enough as we are, we also have the potential to be more. It is about balancing contentment with ambition, acceptance with aspiration.

Embracing innovation is not about becoming someone else or striving for an unattainable ideal. It is about expanding our horizons, pushing our boundaries, and exploring the depths of our potential. It is about seeing every experience, every challenge, every failure as an opportunity to learn, grow, and innovate.

This is not an easy path. It requires courage, resilience, and an open mind. It requires us to step out of our comfort zones, to question our beliefs and assumptions, and to be willing to make mistakes. But the rewards are immense. Embracing innovation leads to personal growth, self-discovery, and a deeper understanding of our true selves.

Innovation is not just about creating new technologies or pioneering scientific research. It is also about challenging societal norms, breaking free from traditional constraints, and redefining our understanding of success. It is about finding new ways to express ourselves, to connect with others, and to make a difference in the world. I am not emphasizing to become rebellious but to carry your brains with you. Use your analysis and knowledge to come to a conclusion. Always remember that what you don't know does not mean that it does not exist. For examples, there are 84000 species of living beings on this earth but you might not know all of them. It requires being humble, compassion, empathy along with the understanding that there should always be a room for healthy conversations.

Innovation, in essence, is a form of self-expression. It is a way of saying, "This is who I am, this is what I believe, and this is what I can do." It is about owning our uniqueness, celebrating our individuality, and using our talents and skills to contribute to the world in our own unique way.

So, while 'You are Enough' is a powerful affirmation of self-acceptance and self-love, it is also a call to action. It is a call to embrace innovation, to embrace our potential, and to embrace the endless possibilities that lie within each one of us.

Embracing innovation does not involve rejecting our identity, but rather, it entails enriching and broadening our potential. It entails acknowledging that although we are sufficient as we are, we also possess the ability to develop, adapt, and undergo a metamorphosis. It involves acknowledging that we are not only sufficient, but also capable of achieving far beyond our current capabilities.

## Exploring New Ideas

In the journey of self-discovery and acceptance, a critical step involves delving into the world of new ideas. It is here, in the realm of the unexplored, that we often find the keys to unlocking our full potential. The beauty of new ideas is that they are like uncharted territory, waiting to be discovered, understood, and eventually applied to our lives.

The exploration of new ideas is not just about the intellectual pursuit but also about the transformation it brings to our lives. It is a process that challenges us, provokes us, and ultimately shapes us into becoming more authentic versions of ourselves. It is about stepping out of our comfort zones, questioning our beliefs, and daring to see the world from a different perspective.

New ideas can be found in various forms and sources. They can be gleaned from books, conversations, experiences, and even from moments of quiet introspection. The point is to remain open, curious, and receptive. It is important to understand that new ideas are not meant to replace our existing beliefs but to enrich them, to add more dimensions to our understanding of ourselves and the world.

Exploring new ideas is not a passive exercise. It requires active engagement, willingness to question, and a desire to learn. It is about challenging our preconceptions, questioning our assumptions, and being open to different viewpoints. It is about embracing the unfamiliar, the unknown, and the unexpected.

In the exploration of new ideas, we often encounter resistance. This resistance can come from within us, from our fears, doubts, and insecurities. It can also come from external sources, from societal norms, expectations, and pressures. However, it is important to remember that resistance is a natural part of the process. It is a sign that we are pushing our boundaries, challenging our comfort zones, and growing as individuals.

The exploration of new ideas is a journey, not a destination. It is a continuous process of learning, growing, and evolving. It is about finding our own paths, discovering our own truths, and creating our own narratives. It is about becoming more aware of our strengths, acknowledging our weaknesses, and embracing our uniqueness.

In the pursuit of new ideas, we often find ourselves. We discover our passions, our values, and our purpose. We uncover our potential, our capabilities, and our possibilities. We realize that we are enough, just as we are.

So, let us embrace the exploration of new ideas. Let us be bold, be curious, and be open. Let us challenge ourselves, push our boundaries, and step out of our comfort zones. Let us explore, discover, and grow. For in the exploration of new ideas, we find not only the keys to unlocking our full potential but also the path to self-discovery, acceptance, and ultimately, self-love.

Remember, the exploration of new ideas is not about becoming someone else. It is about becoming the best version of ourselves. It is about realizing that we are enough, just as we are. So, let us explore, let us discover, and let us grow. For in the end, we are all works in progress, on a journey of becoming more of who we truly are.

## Expressing Through Art

The world of art is a vast, unlimited universe, brimming with the potential to express our deepest emotions, our wildest dreams, and our most profound thoughts. It provides an avenue for us to express what we might otherwise struggle to communicate through words alone. Art, in its multitude of forms, is a powerful tool for self-expression and self-discovery, a medium through which we can explore the depths of our being and affirm our belief that we are enough.

As you immerse yourself in the world of art, you begin a journey of self-discovery. Whether it's through painting, sketching, sculpting, dancing, writing, or any other art form, you give yourself the chance to discover and explore parts of yourself you might have otherwise overlooked. It's a process that allows you to delve into your thoughts, feelings, and experiences, helping you gain a deeper understanding of yourself.

Art is a mirror reflecting your inner world. It's an external manifestation of your internal landscape. Each stroke of paint, each movement of dance, each word written down, is a piece of you. It's a testament to your experiences, your emotions, your thoughts, your dreams, and your fears. It's a testament to your authenticity, your uniqueness, and your individuality. It's a testament to the fact that you are enough.

The beauty of art lies not only in the end product but also in the process. It's in the journey of creation where the magic truly happens. Each step in the process, from the initial spark of inspiration to the final touches, is a moment of self-expression, a moment of self-discovery, and a moment of self-affirmation. It's a moment where you tell yourself and the world that you are enough.

The act of creating art is an act of courage. It's about daring to express yourself in your truest form, daring to be vulnerable, daring to be authentic, and daring to believe in your worth. It's about stepping outside of your comfort zone, pushing your boundaries, and challenging your beliefs. It's about embracing your individuality and celebrating your uniqueness. It's about embracing the belief that you are enough.

Art is a journey, a journey of self-discovery, a journey of self-expression, and a journey of self-affirmation. It's a journey that allows you to explore the depths of your being, express your authentic self, and affirm your belief that you are enough. It's a journey that allows you to connect with your emotions, your thoughts, your dreams, and your fears. It's a journey that allows you to connect with yourself on a deeper level.

Through art, you can express yourself in ways words might fail to. You can convey your emotions, your thoughts, your dreams, and your fears in a tangible form. You can communicate your experiences, your perspective, and your worldview.

Art is not about perfection, it's about expression. It's not about comparing yourself to others, it's about expressing your authentic self. It's not about meeting external standards; it's about meeting your own. It's not about seeking validation from others; it's about affirming your belief in your worth.

In the end, art is a celebration of who you are. It's a celebration of your emotions, your thoughts, your experiences, your dreams, and your fears. It's a celebration of your authenticity, your individuality, and your uniqueness. And most importantly, it's a celebration of the fact that you are enough. Through art, you express yourself, you discover yourself and your true potential.

## Cultivating Curiosity

As we journey through the pages of self-acceptance and self-love, it is impossible to ignore a key ingredient that fuels our self-discovery - curiosity. The power of curiosity is often underestimated yet it is this very quality that allows us to explore who we are, what we want and where we are going.

Curiosity, a trait inherent in all of us, is like a compass guiding us towards our true selves. It is the spark that ignites exploration, learning, and growth. It is what propels us to question, to probe, and to seek understanding. Curiosity has the power to open our minds, broaden our perspectives, and deepen our understanding of ourselves and the world around us.

When we allow our curiosity to flourish, we cultivate a mindset that is open, inquisitive, and eager for knowledge. We become active participants in our own lives, keen to learn and grow. We start questioning the status quo, challenging our own beliefs and assumptions, and seeking new experiences and perspectives. This is the essence of self-discovery.

Curiosity, however, is not just about seeking new experiences or knowledge. It is also about embracing the unknown, the uncertain, and the unfamiliar. It is about being comfortable with questions, with not knowing, and with the process of discovery. It is about being open to surprises, to learning, and to change.

Curiosity is a process that involves questioning, exploring, learning, and growing. It is a never-ending journey of discovery, of getting to know ourselves better, and of understanding the world around us. The more we nurture our curiosity, the more we become aware of our own potential and the possibilities that life has to offer.

But how do we cultivate curiosity? The first step is to embrace it. We need to give ourselves permission to be curious, to ask questions, to explore, and to seek understanding. We need to let go of our fear of the unknown, of failure, or of looking foolish. We need to be open to new experiences, to learning, and to change.

The second step is to nurture it. We can do this by creating an environment that encourages curiosity for ourselves and others. This can be as simple as reading a book, taking a class, learning new skill, or exploring a new place. It can also involve more complex activities such as engaging in challenging conversations, solving problems, or pursuing creative endeavors.

The third step is to practice it. Like any other skill, curiosity can be developed and strengthened through practice. This means deliberately seeking out opportunities to learn, to explore, and to question. It means being open-minded, being willing to change our minds, and being comfortable with uncertainty. It is more about being flexible to new experiences of life and going deeper to understand them.

In conclusion, cultivating curiosity is a vital part of our journey towards self-acceptance and self-love. It is what allows us to explore who we are, what we want, and where we are going. It is what empowers us to learn, to grow, and to become the best version of ourselves. So, let's embrace curiosity, nurture it, and practice it. Let's cultivate curiosity and discover the endless possibilities that lie within us.

# Chapter 12: Fostering Connections

## Building Relationships

As we traverse the intricate maze of existence, we gradually comprehend that our connections with others are not merely fortuitous, but rather indispensable. The relationships we build, nurture, and maintain become the bridges between our individual worlds, the conduit through which we share our experiences, our thoughts, and our hopes. They are the lifelines that connect us to the essence of humanity – to love, to understanding, to compassion, to share and to care. IT can be your mom, dad, sister, in-laws, kids, friends or anyone one this planet, it can be your pet also. The relationship flourishes when we are unconditional, non-judgmental and true to every aspect of that bond.

To attract beautiful relationships in our life can be done by giving unconditional love to every relation we have in our life. The one who are meant for you will always stay with you and the rest will be leaving you for one reason or the other. But the only condition to have good relationships in our life is to spread truly unconditional love and care.

Building relationships, then, is not a task to be taken lightly. It is a responsibility that demands our time, our energy, and most importantly, our authenticity. We are not islands, isolated and independent. We are, in fact, interconnected beings, each of us a part of a larger whole. And it is in recognizing this interconnection that we begin to understand the importance of building relationships based on mutual respect, empathy, and kindness.

Reflecting upon my own experiences has illuminated the necessity of this understanding. I have found that the most fulfilling relationships in my life have been those in which I have been able to be my true self, unencumbered by the weight of pretense or the fear of judgment. In these relationships, I have felt seen, heard, and valued – not for what I can do or what I have, but for who I am.

Yet, the path to building such relationships is not always clear. It is a path fraught with challenges and obstacles, with misunderstandings and miscommunications. It requires patience, perseverance, and a willingness to be accessible. It requires us to confront our own insecurities and prejudices, to question our assumptions and beliefs, and to open our minds and hearts to the perspectives and experiences of others.

In building relationships, we must also recognize the importance of boundaries. While it is essential to be open and vulnerable, it is equally important to protect our own emotional and mental well-being. Healthy relationships are not built on coercion or manipulation, but on mutual consent and respect. They require us to respect not only the boundaries of others but also our own.

Building relationships is a continuous process, a journey rather than a destination. It is a journey that demands our presence, our attention, and our commitment. It is a journey that challenges us to grow, to evolve, and to become better versions of ourselves.

Building relationships, then, is not about becoming something more, but about recognizing and honoring our inherent worth our ourselves. It is about seeing and being seen, about hearing and being heard, about understanding and being understood. Building relationships with others is not hindered by our imperfections; rather, it is enhanced by them. Embracing the complexities of human existence and sharing our vulnerabilities with others is what truly matters.

So, as we navigate the complexities of building relationships, let us remember that we are enough. Let us remember to be authentic, to be kind, to be respectful. Let us remember to be patient, to be understanding, to be compassionate. But most importantly, let us remember to be ourselves, for it is in our authenticity that we build the most meaningful and fulfilling relationships. Building healthy relationships does not involve forming emotional dependencies in order to find happiness or satisfaction through using others to fulfill tasks. It is not about exploiting others for personal gain. These types of connections often lead to feelings of emptiness and require a significant amount of energy, as they are rooted in selfish needs.

Always keep in mind that once you are content with yourself, you are prepared to be selfless, willing to offer more without expecting anything in return. This is when genuine relationships thrive and prosper, bringing immense joy and unity.

## Communicating Effectively

In our journey towards self-acceptance and understanding that we are enough, we must not forget the importance of effective communication. It is through clear, precise, and empathetic exchanges that we nourish our relationships and connect with others on a deeper level. This is not just about speaking and being heard but also about listening and understanding.

The essence of communication lies in its two-way nature. While it is vital to express our feelings, thoughts, and ideas, it is equally crucial to listen to what others have to say. Listening allows us to gain a better understanding of their perspectives and contexts, fostering empathy and mutual respect. It is a reminder that everyone has their unique journeys and narratives, and acknowledging them can be a powerful way of saying, "You are enough, and I see that."

Effective communication also requires clarity and precision. It's not enough to assume that our message is understood as we intended. We must strive to express ourselves in a manner that leaves no room for misinterpretation. This involves simplifying complex ideas, choosing our words carefully, and using non-verbal cues to reinforce our message. Clarity in communication not only minimizes misunderstandings but also fosters trust and openness in our interactions.

However, communicating effectively is not just about what we say or how we say it. It's also about the space we create for these conversations. A safe, non-judgmental space allows everyone involved to express themselves freely and honestly. It encourages vulnerability, which is a cornerstone of deep, meaningful connections. In such spaces, we can share our fears, joys, dreams, and disappointments without the fear of being judged or misunderstood. We can say, "This is me, in all my glory and imperfections," and know that we will be accepted.

As we strive to communicate more effectively, we must also be mindful of our emotional intelligence. This involves recognizing, understanding, and managing not just our emotions but also those of others. It is about being sensitive to the emotional undercurrents in our interactions and responding to them with empathy and understanding. Emotional intelligence can guide us towards more compassionate and respectful communication, fostering stronger, more fulfilling relationships.

There is an inherent power in effective communication, a power that can transform our relationships and our perception of self. It is a tool that, when used correctly, can help us understand and accept not just others but also ourselves. It can help us navigate the complexities of human interactions, bridging gaps and fostering understanding.

Remember, communication is not a one-size-fits-all approach. It requires constant learning, unlearning, and relearning. It involves adapting to different people and situations, understanding their unique needs and contexts. It is a continuous journey of growth and evolution, much like our journey towards realizing that we are enough.

So, as we continue to embrace our worthiness, let's also strive to communicate more effectively. Let's listen with empathy, speak with clarity, and create safe spaces for honest conversations. Let's use our words and our silence to say, "I see you, I hear you, and you are magnificent in your own way." This is the power of communicating effectively, a vital step in our journey towards self-acceptance and self-love.

## Understanding Others

As we navigate the intricate path of self-exploration and embracing who we truly are, we eventually find ourselves standing at the entrance of empathy. We are not isolated beings. We exist in a web of relationships, and it's through understanding others that we can deepen our understanding of ourselves. This chapter serves as a guide to building that bridge of empathy towards others, which in turn reinforces our sense of self-worth.

When we talk about understanding others, we're not just addressing the surface-level knowledge of their likes and dislikes. It's about delving deeper, acknowledging their fears, aspirations, struggles, and triumphs. It's about recognizing that every person we encounter carries a universe within them, rich with experiences and emotions that have shaped them into who they are today.

The first step towards understanding others is active listening. We often listen to respond, not to understand. We're eager to interject our opinions or advice, neglecting the fact that sometimes, all a person needs is someone to listen, and just listen without any judgments or advice. Active listening involves fully immersing ourselves in the other person's narrative, setting aside our judgments and preconceptions. It's about making them feel heard and validated.

Understanding others also requires us to exercise empathy. Empathy is the ability to step into someone else's shoes, to feel their emotions and see the world from their perspective. It's important to remember that empathy doesn't necessarily mean agreement. It's entirely possible to empathize with someone even if we don't agree with their actions or decisions. Empathy is about understanding, not endorsing.

Developing empathy becomes easier when we embrace the fact that every person is unique. We all have different backgrounds, experiences, and perspectives that shape our worldview. No two people are the same, and it's this diversity that adds richness to our collective human experience. By embracing this variety, we enhance our ability to comprehend the drives and sentiments of those in our midst. This enables us to coexist peacefully with all individuals in our surroundings and within our personal sphere filled with completeness and feelings.

Moreover, understanding others requires patience. People are complex, and it takes time to unravel the layers of their personality. It's about investing time and energy into building genuine relationships, being there for them in their moments of vulnerability, and celebrating their victories.

As we grow in understanding others, we also grow in understanding ourselves. We start to see our prejudices, biases, and assumptions. We become more aware of our strengths and areas of growth. We learn to love and accept ourselves, warts and all. We realize that just like others, we too are a work in progress, continually evolving and growing.

In understanding others, we also learn the power of compassion. We realize that everyone is fighting their own battles, some visible, others hidden. We learn to be kind, not just to others but also to ourselves. We understand that it's okay to make mistakes, to have bad days, to not have all the answers.

Understanding others is an essential element in the fabric of life. It brings enrichment to our existence, strengthens our connections with others, and fosters a greater sense of self-awareness. It's a journey that requires patience, empathy, and open-mindedness. But the rewards are immeasurable.

Remember, you are enough. Your journey, your growth, your understanding of others and yourself, is a testament to your strength and resilience. Embrace it, celebrate it, and continue to grow. Because the world needs more people who understand, empathize, and love.

## Practicing Empathy

In our voyage of self-discovery and acceptance, we must acknowledge the crucial role empathy plays. It is more than just a virtue; it is a tool, a bridge that connects us to others, enabling us to understand their feelings, experiences, and perspectives. Empathy is not an innate trait. It necessitates dedication, perseverance, and purposeful effort.

When we begin to practice empathy, we start by listening, truly listening to others. This involves silencing our own thoughts, judgments, and advice, and focusing entirely on the other person, their words, emotions and underlying messages. It's not about coming up with a solution or a quick fix, but about validating their feelings and making them feel heard and understood. This can be challenging, as it often goes against our instinct to problem-solve or make things better.

Practicing empathy requires us to embrace the perspectives and emotions of others, while maintaining an accepting and open-minded attitude. This means stepping out of our comfort zone, challenging our preconceived notions, and embracing diversity in all its forms. It's about seeing the world through someone else's eyes, even if their perspective is vastly different from our own. This is where empathy becomes transformative, not just for the other person, but for us as well.

It's important to remember that empathy is not about losing ourselves in the feelings of others. It is about understanding and sharing their feelings while maintaining our own boundaries. It's about being compassionate without compromising our own well-being. This balance can be tricky to maintain, but it is essential for healthy empathy.

As we practice empathy, we also need to practice self-empathy. This involves acknowledging our own feelings, giving ourselves permission to feel, and treating ourselves with kindness and understanding. We often neglect this aspect of empathy, but it is just as important. After all, how can we truly empathize with others if we can't do the same for ourselves?

Developing empathy can be challenging on an emotional level. It necessitates being open, brave, and strong. However, the benefits are significant. Empathy fosters connection, builds trust, and promotes mutual understanding. It can bridge gaps, mend relationships, and even heal deep-seated wounds. It is a powerful force for change, both at a personal and societal level.

In a world that often feels divided and disconnected, empathy is more important than ever. It reminds us of our shared humanity, our interconnectedness, and our capacity for compassion and kindness. It teaches us to celebrate our differences, rather than fear them. It encourages us to be more open, more understanding, and more accepting of others.

Practicing empathy is an ongoing journey. It is a skill that we can always improve, a capacity that we can always expand. It requires effort, mindfulness, and a willingness to grow. But the journey is worth it, for in practicing empathy, we not only become better friends, partners, and community members, but we also become more accepting and loving versions of ourselves.

In the end, practicing empathy is about becoming more human. It's about recognizing and honoring the inherent worth and dignity of all people, including ourselves. It's about realizing that we are all imperfect, all struggling, all trying our best. And in this realization, we find that we are enough, just as we are.

## Embracing Diversity

Within the vast canvas of life, we are delicately intertwined strands of various hues, patterns, and sizes, each contributing a special element to the complete work of art. The beauty of our world lies in its diversity, a myriad of cultures, beliefs, and perspectives that enrich our collective experience and deepen our understanding of the world around us. Yet, in our pursuit of sameness, we often fail to appreciate the value of this diversity.

We live in an age where individuality is often overshadowed by mass culture, where conformity is prized over uniqueness. We are often taught to blend in, to conform to societal norms and expectations. This is a narrative that we have been told, one that has been ingrained in us from a young age. But is it not our differences that spark innovation, that inspire creativity, that drive evolution? The answer is a resounding yes.

Embracing diversity is not just about recognizing and respecting our differences. It is about understanding that each of us, in our own unique way, is enough. It is about acknowledging that our diversity is our strength, that our differences do not divide us, but rather, they unite us. It is about seeing the beauty in our individual uniqueness and celebrating it. It is about accepting ourselves and others for who we are, without judgment or prejudice.

Too often, we compare ourselves to others, measuring our worth by how closely we align with societal ideals. We strive for perfection, only to realize that it is an elusive, unattainable goal. We are not perfect, and that is okay. We are human. We are diverse. We are beautiful in our own unique ways. We are enough.

When we embrace diversity, we create a world where everyone feels seen, heard, and valued. We foster a sense of belonging, where people can show up as their true, authentic selves without fear of judgment or rejection. We cultivate empathy and understanding, breaking down barriers and building bridges between cultures, communities, and individuals.

Embracing diversity also means challenging our own biases and prejudices. It means stepping out of our comfort zones, opening our minds, and seeking to understand perspectives that differ from our own. It means recognizing and challenging systems of oppression, discrimination, and inequality. It means standing up for justice, equality, and human rights.

In embracing diversity, we find unity. We discover that beneath our external differences, we share a common humanity. We may come from different backgrounds, religions or culture, or we might have different experiences, and hold different beliefs, but at our core, we are all human. We all seek love, happiness, and fulfillment. We all strive to live meaningful lives. We all have dreams, hopes, and fears. We all have stories to tell.

In the end, embracing diversity is about more than just tolerating differences. It is about celebrating them. It is about learning from them. It is about growing from them. It is about creating a world where everyone, regardless of their race, religion, gender, sexuality, age, or ability, feels valued, respected, and enough.

So let us embrace diversity. Let us celebrate our individual uniqueness. Let us learn from each other. Let us grow together. Let us create a world where everyone feels enough. Because we are enough in our own way.

# Chapter 13: Living in Harmony

## Respecting Nature

As I gently walk through the nature, the sun's rays filtering through the rustling leaves, I am struck by an overwhelming sense of awe. The complexity and beauty of the natural world humbles me. Nature is not merely a backdrop to our human drama, but a living entity in itself that demands our respect. It is in this context that I reflect on the significance of respecting nature and everything that nature is giving us.

Respecting the natural world extends beyond simply appreciating its magnificence and abundance. It entails a deep understanding of our role within the vast interconnectedness of existence. We are not superior to nature; we are a part of it. We are interdependent with all life forms and our actions inevitably impact the environment. This realization calls for a paradigm shift in our approach. We must move from exploitation to coexistence, from dominance to stewardship.

As I watch the fluttering butterflies, the industrious ants, the towering trees, and the vibrant flowers, I am reminded of the majestic mosaic of life. Each organism, no matter how small or seemingly insignificant, plays a critical role in maintaining the equilibrium of our ecosystem. Respecting nature is acknowledging this interconnectivity and valuing each life form for its unique contribution.

While our technological advancements have made our lives more comfortable, they have also distanced us from nature. We live in concrete jungles, oblivious to the rhythms of the natural world. Our relentless pursuit of progress has led to the degradation of our environment, threatening our own survival. Respecting nature means recognizing the limits of our exploitation and learning to live sustainably.

To clarify, I encountered a situation where numerous red ants invaded my kitchen, causing chaos in search of food. Despite their small size, their bites were quite discomforting. Typically, they are found in kitchens when even a small amount of food is left on shelves or anywhere in the house. Continuing from where I left off, I attempted various methods to keep them out of my kitchen and home. However, without pest control at home, they quickly find a way inside. Eventually, I realized they were seeking food, so I decided to provide them with food near their nest to prevent them from attacking my living area. They were simply looking to survive and avoid my space for that very reason. Living on the 10th floor, it was surprising to see red ants attempting to reach such heights. To my amazement, my strategy worked. By placing food near their nest, they stopped entering my kitchen. The lesson learned from this experience is that we must respect their living space and not disrupt their comfort zone. This is just one example involving small red ants, but there are countless instances where animals suffer due to human interference in the name of development. Our focus on meeting their needs has led us to become increasingly detached from our own humanity. Similarly, we can apply this concept to the discussion of natural resources.

In our hectic lives, we often forget to pause and appreciate the serenity and healing that nature offers. The rustling of leaves, the chirping of birds, the gurgling of a brook, the fragrance of flowers, the taste of fresh fruits - these are not just sensory experiences but a way to connect with our inner selves. Respecting nature is about nurturing this connection and allowing nature to nourish our souls.

As I gaze at the star-studded sky, I am reminded of the vastness of the universe and the transience of our existence. The natural world, with its cyclic patterns of birth, growth, decay, and renewal, teaches us the impermanence of life. Respecting nature is embracing these truths and living in harmony with them.

In the end, respecting nature is not just about preserving it for future generations, but also about enhancing our own existence. It is about realizing that we are enough - that we don't need to constantly strive for more at the cost of our environment. It is about finding contentment in the simplicity and beauty of nature.

Indeed, the respect we accord to nature is a reflection of our self-respect. By respecting nature, we are respecting ourselves, our interdependence with all life forms, and our place in the universe. Our relationship with nature is a mirror to our relationship with ourselves.

As I leave the nature walk, I carry with me a renewed sense of reverence for nature. I am reminded of the words of the

Native American Chief Seattle, "Man does not weave this web of life. He is merely a strand in it. Whatever he does to the web, he does to himself." Respecting nature, thus, is not just an act of conservation, but an act of self-realization and self-preservation. It is a journey towards understanding that we are enough.

## Promoting Peace

In the journey of self-discovery and acceptance, it is crucial to understand the role that peace plays in our lives. Peace is not merely the absence of conflict, but the presence of harmony, tranquility, and serenity. It is a state of mind and an approach to life that requires conscious effort to achieve and maintain. When we embrace peace, we are essentially opening up to the possibility of a life less burdened by stress, conflict, and negativity.

Promoting peace begins with the self. It is the realization that you are, in your most basic form, a vessel of peace. It is the acceptance of your innate capacity to cultivate peace within yourself and extend it to others. The journey towards peace is an inward one, a profound exploration of the self that begins with the acceptance of your inherent worth. You are, after all, enough. You are a complete entity, capable of giving and receiving love, capable of growth, and capable of promoting peace.

The journey towards peace is not an easy one. It requires the courage to confront your fears, insecurities, and doubts. It requires the willingness to let go of the past, of the hurts and disappointments that have shaped your perception of yourself and the world around you. It requires the strength to forgive, not only others but also yourself. Forgiveness is a powerful tool in promoting peace. It allows you to free yourself from the chains of resentment and bitterness, allowing you to move forward with a lighter heart and a clearer mind.

Promoting peace also involves the cultivation of positive attitudes and behaviors. It is about choosing kindness over cruelty, understanding over judgment, and love over hate. It is about treating others with respect and dignity, regardless of their race, religion, gender, or social status. It is about being mindful of your thoughts, words, and actions, ensuring that they are in alignment with the values of peace and harmony.

Promoting peace is not a solitary endeavor. It is a collective effort that involves everyone. Each one of us has a role to play in creating a peaceful world. This starts with our families, our friends, our communities, and extends to our workplaces, our societies, and the world at large. It is about fostering a culture of peace, where differences are celebrated, conflicts are resolved through dialogue, and everyone is treated with fairness and justice.

Promoting peace is a lifelong commitment. It is not a destination, but a journey, a continuous process of learning, growing, and evolving. It is about constantly striving to be better, to do better, and to create a better world for ourselves and future generations. It is about recognizing that peace is not a luxury, but a necessity, a fundamental human right that everyone deserves.

In conclusion, promoting peace is an integral part of the journey towards self-discovery and acceptance. It is about recognizing your worth, embracing your capacity for love and growth, and using these to create a positive impact in the world. Remember, you are enough, and you have the power to promote peace.

## Embracing Interconnectedness

In our journey towards self-acceptance and self-love, we often overlook the importance of interconnectedness. It's easy to get lost in the narrative of 'me' and 'I', forgetting that we are intrinsically linked to the world around us. Our lives are not lived in isolation; they are like a beautiful tapestry, woven with intricate connections, shared moments, and mutual inspirations.

Understanding and embracing this interconnectedness is a significant step towards realizing that we are enough. It allows us to see ourselves not as isolated beings struggling alone, but as part of a larger whole, contributing and receiving in equal measures. It's a shift from a self-centered perspective to a broader, more inclusive worldview.

Consider, for instance, the air we breathe. It's not 'ours' in the possessive sense. The oxygen we inhale has likely been part of countless other beings before reaching us. It's a part of a cycle, a system that we are just one component of. Similarly, our actions and choices have ripples that extend far beyond our immediate surroundings. We are not islands; we are part of an interconnected world.

Embracing this interconnectedness also helps us see the inherent value in ourselves and others. When we understand that every person, every creature, every element in this world plays a vital role in maintaining the balance of life, we begin to appreciate our own worth. We are enough, not solely due to our individual existence, but rather because we form an essential component of this magnificent interconnected web of existence.

This realization can have profound implications on our mental and emotional well-being. It can alleviate feelings of loneliness and isolation, reminding us that we are never truly alone. We are part of a community, a species, an ecosystem, a universe. Our struggles and triumphs are shared, our joys and sorrows echoed in countless other hearts.

Moreover, embracing interconnectedness fosters empathy and compassion. When we see ourselves as part of a larger whole, we become more aware of the impact of our actions on others. We become more attuned to the needs and feelings of those around us, fostering a sense of shared responsibility and mutual care.

However, acknowledging our interconnectedness doesn't mean losing our individuality. It's not about dissolving into a faceless mass, but about recognizing that our unique selves are part of something bigger. It's about finding our place in the world, understanding our role, and appreciating our worth.

This is not an easy shift to make. It requires introspection, openness, and a willingness to see beyond the boundaries of our own existence. But the rewards are immense. Embracing interconnectedness can bring a sense of peace, belonging, and purpose. It can help us realize that we are not just enough, but that we are integral to the world around us.

So, let's expand our perspective. Let's see ourselves not just as individuals, but as threads in a beautiful, complex, and interconnected tapestry of life. Let's celebrate our individuality while acknowledging our shared existence. Let's embrace our interconnectedness and realize that we are, indeed, enough.

## Fostering Global Unity

Within the fabric of vigor, our connections are woven together in a harmonious symphony. Each thread of our existence, no matter how seemingly insignificant, weaves into the larger fabric of our global society. As we delve deeper into understanding our individual worth, it becomes apparent that our collective value is just as significant. This chapter invites us to explore the concept of global unity and how our individual sense of being enough can contribute to fostering a more united and harmonious world.

The concept of global unity can sometimes feel abstract and distant, especially in a world that often seems fragmented and divided. Yet, it is in acknowledging our shared humanity that we start to see the threads that bind us together. We are all human beings, each with our unique stories, dreams, and struggles, yet all sharing the same home - Earth. In recognizing this, we begin to see that our actions, no matter how small, can have a ripple effect, touching lives far beyond our immediate sphere.

Embracing the realization that we are sufficient in our current state allows us to share this mindset with others, fostering a culture of inclusivity and admiration. This does not mean that we must agree on everything or that conflicts will suddenly vanish. Rather, it means that we can approach differences with empathy, recognizing that each person's perspective is valid and shaped by their unique experiences.

Moreover, feeling enough within ourselves can empower us to make positive changes in the world. Often, feelings of inadequacy can lead to inaction - we may feel that we are too insignificant to make a difference. However, when we truly embrace our worth, we realize that every action counts. Each kind word spoken, each hand extended in help, each step taken towards understanding - they all matter. They all contribute to the global unity.

In fostering global unity, it's essential to remember that unity does not mean uniformity. We are a world of diverse cultures, beliefs, and perspectives, and these differences should be celebrated, not suppressed. Global unity is about embracing this diversity and finding common ground amidst our differences. It's about recognizing our shared humanity and working towards a world where everyone feels valued and enough.

However, fostering global unity is not a task for a few. It requires the collective effort of all of us. It begins with each of us embracing our individual worth and extending this acceptance to others. It involves making conscious choices that promote understanding and respect. It means standing up against prejudice and discrimination and working towards a more equitable world.

In conclusion, fostering global unity is both a personal and collective journey. It starts with the understanding that we are enough and extends to the belief that everyone else is too. It's about recognizing our shared humanity, celebrating our diversity, and working towards a world where everyone feels seen, heard, and valued. It's a journey worth embarking on, for in unity, we find not only peace but also the potential for a better, more compassionate world. So, let us all weave our threads into the tapestry of global unity, for each thread matters, each thread counts, and each thread is enough.

## Contributing To Sustainability

As we journey through the chapters of self-discovery and personal growth, it becomes increasingly evident that our individual actions and choices have a far-reaching impact. The realization that we are not isolated entities, but rather interconnected beings in a vast and intricate ecosystem, brings us to the pivotal concept of sustainability. In this context, sustainability refers to the mindful utilization of resources to meet our needs while ensuring the well-being of future generations.

When we talk about sustainability, we often think of it in grandiose terms, as something that requires colossal efforts and extensive lifestyle changes. However, the truth is, contributing to sustainability can start from the smallest of actions and decisions we make daily. It can be as simple as choosing to recycle, conserving water, or opting for public transportation instead of private vehicles. It's simply contributing with small endeavors to become part of huge cause.

In my journey of embracing my wholeness and learning to believe that I am enough, I found that this understanding of sustainability is closely linked to self-worth. It is about realizing that we have a responsibility towards our planet and future generations, and that our actions, no matter how small, can make a difference.

I remember a time when I felt overwhelmed and powerless in the face of the immense environmental challenges our world is facing. It seemed like the problem was too big, and I was too small. But as I delved deeper into my journey of self-discovery, I realized that this mindset was a reflection of my own feelings of inadequacy. I was projecting my own belief of not being enough onto the situation. And believe me corona has taught us that we don't need much to live a happy and contented life.

Embracing the belief that I am enough allowed me to see that I do have power, that my actions do matter. I started making small changes in my lifestyle, like reducing waste, recycling more, and being mindful of my energy consumption. I found that these actions not only contributed to sustainability but also nurtured my sense of self-worth.

For instance, choosing to use a reusable shopping bag instead of a plastic one wasn't just about reducing plastic waste. It was also a statement that I care about the environment, that I am taking responsibility, and that I am enough to make a difference.

Likewise, deciding to consume less and live a more minimalist lifestyle wasn't just about saving resources. It was also about asserting my belief that I don't need to constantly acquire more to feel worthy or fulfilled. I am enough as I am.

Contributing to sustainability, therefore, is not just about preserving the environment. It's about fostering a mindset of abundance and worthiness. We don't need to constantly consume and deplete our planet's resources to feel satisfied or complete. More connections with nature is important as nature teaches us many things.

This realization has been empowering. It has allowed me to shed feelings of helplessness and take positive action. It has made me understand that contributing to sustainability is not a burden, but a privilege and a responsibility that comes with being a part of this beautiful, interconnected web of life.

In conclusion, embracing our enough-ness can transform the way we relate to our planet and our resources. It can empower us to make choices that not only benefit the environment but also reinforce our sense of self-worth and fulfillment. Because, in the end, we are enough, and our actions matter.

# Chapter 14: Embracing Spirituality

## Understanding Spirituality

While navigating the twists and turns of life, we frequently come across ourselves at the intersection of profound questions. The quest for meaning, the need to know our purpose, the longing to connect with something larger than ourselves, these all usher us towards the realm of spirituality. It is not a realm bound by the rules of physical reality, but a domain where the soul finds its voice and the heart its home. And I have found mine.

Understanding spirituality is akin to decoding the language of the soul. It's not about adhering to a particular religion or following a prescribed set of rituals. Instead, it's about exploring our inner selves and seeking our own personal truth. Spirituality is deeply personal and unique to each individual, like a fingerprint, marking our unique connection to the universe.

Spirituality elicits a sense of interconnectedness, a realization that we are not isolated entities, but integral parts of a grand cosmic universe. It fosters a sense of unity, dissolving the boundaries that divide us and nurturing empathy, compassion, and kindness. It is the recognition that despite our differences, we share a common human experience, and our individual stories are simply different chapters in the book of humanity.

As we delve into spirituality, we come to understand that it is a path that leads us to a deeper understanding of ourselves and the world around us. It is about finding our place in the universe and understanding our role in the grand scheme of things.

Spirituality also encourages us to look beyond the material world and seek fulfillment in the intangible. It teaches us to find joy in the simple things, to appreciate the beauty in the ordinary, and to find peace in the silence. It is about learning to live in the moment, to be fully present, and to experience life in all its richness.

At its core, spirituality is about love. It is about cultivating a love for ourselves, for others, and for the universe. It is about recognizing that we are all part of the same divine essence, and that love is the thread that binds us all together.

Understanding spirituality also involves acknowledging our own imperfections and embracing our vulnerabilities. It invites us to face our fears, to confront our shadows, and to use these experiences as catalysts for growth. It is about learning to accept ourselves as we are, with all our flaws and imperfections, and realizing that we are enough.

In essence, spirituality is the journey of the soul. It is the exploration of the inner universe, the quest for self-discovery, and the pursuit of personal truth. Discovering our individual journey and navigating it with bravery, genuineness, and affection. It involves accepting our human nature, honoring our spiritual essence, and recognizing that we are truly sufficient as ourselves.

In the end, understanding spirituality is not about finding the answers, but about asking the right questions. It is about daring to dive into the depths of our being, to explore the mysteries of the soul, and to discover the limitless potential that lies within us all. It is about finding the courage to be ourselves, to live our truth, and to embrace individuality.

## Exploring Beliefs

Exploring our beliefs is a significant part of the journey towards self-discovery. These beliefs form the core principles that influence how we see the world and our role in it. They act as the hidden roots of a tree, grounding us in our existence, even when we are unaware of their presence.

Our beliefs are formed and influenced by a complex interplay of factors; our upbringing, societal norms, culture, religion, experiences, and even the books we read. They are deeply embedded within us, often to such an extent that we may not even recognize them as beliefs. Instead, we might perceive them as inherent truths about ourselves and the world.

Our beliefs can be empowering, fueling our passion, and driving us towards our goals. They can give us a sense of purpose, a reason to persevere, a sense of belonging. However, they can also be limiting, holding us back from realizing our full potential. They can make us feel stuck, unworthy, or fearful. And so, it becomes essential to delve into the depths of our beliefs, to understand them, question them, and reshape them if needed.

Reflecting upon our beliefs can be an enlightening experience, akin to peeling back the layers of an onion. Each layer may reveal a new facet of our belief system, each one more profound than the last. The process may even evoke a range of emotions - surprise, confusion, resistance, or even an overwhelming sense of liberation.

One of the most powerful beliefs that we often grapple with is the belief about our own worthiness. The belief that we are enough. This belief, or the lack thereof, can significantly impact our self-esteem, our relationships, and our ability to pursue our dreams. If our internal narrative continually echoes the sentiment that we are not enough, we may find ourselves trapped in a cycle of self-doubt and self-sabotage. Due to this inherent characteristic, we have developed numerous dependencies on others. Additionally, we often become victims of various unfortunate events and manipulative campaigns, where our lack of self-esteem and shortcomings are exploited to target us. In fact, when our belief system is not strong, one can take advantage of that to play with your values and emotions.

Conversely, when we nurture the belief that we are enough, we allow ourselves to embrace our imperfections, to be authentic, to love ourselves unconditionally. We permit ourselves to dream big, to take risks, to step out of our comfort zones. We acknowledge our inherent worth, independent of our achievements, our failures, our strengths, or our weaknesses.

But how do we cultivate this belief? How do we uproot the deep-seated beliefs that no longer serve us and plant new ones that empower us? The answer lies in self-awareness and self-compassion. We must first recognize our limiting beliefs, understand their origins, and acknowledge the impact they have had on our lives. We must then gently challenge these beliefs, replacing them with affirmations of self-worth and self-love.

The process of exploring our beliefs may be challenging, uncomfortable, even painful at times. But the rewards are immeasurable. For in the exploration of our beliefs, we not only discover our true selves, but we also pave the way for a life of authenticity, fulfillment, and inner peace. A life where we truly believe that we are enough. It is a testament to our resilience, our strength, and our commitment to living our truth. So, embark on this journey with an open heart and an open mind.

## Nurturing Inner Peace

In life's ceaseless whirlwind, the quest for serenity often feels like an elusive pursuit. It's not found in the outside world, but within the depths of our inner selves. It's in this peaceful haven where we discover our own worth, where we truly understand that we are enough.

Nurturing inner peace is akin to tending a garden. It requires patience, dedication, and the understanding that some days will be stormy, others radiant. It is not about resisting life's tempests but learning to dance in the rain, knowing that even in the midst of chaos, tranquility resides within us, waiting to be awakened.

The first step towards nurturing inner peace is acceptance. Acceptance of self, acceptance of others, acceptance of life in all its beautiful complexities. It is about understanding that we are not defined by our mistakes, our past, or our fears. We are enough, not because of what we have done or what we own, but because of who we are - unique, irreplaceable beings, each with a distinctive purpose. Embrace your imperfections, for they create the mosaic that is you.

Next, we need to cultivate mindfulness. Being present, truly present, is a fundamental aspect of inner peace. It is about finding joy in the ordinary, about recognizing that every moment is a gift to be cherished. In the rush to reach various milestones, we often overlook the beauty of the journey. Mindfulness is the gentle reminder to slow down, to breathe, to live. It is about realizing that we are not just human beings, but human 'becomings', in a constant state of evolution.

Forgiveness is another crucial element in this journey. It is about releasing the burdens of resentment and letting go of grudges. It is about understanding that forgiveness is not a sign of weakness, but of strength. It is not about forgetting, but about learning and growing. Forgiveness is the key that unlocks the door to inner peace.

Moreover, inner peace is nurtured through gratitude. Gratitude shifts our focus from what we lack to what we have. It is the recognition of the abundance that surrounds us. It is about appreciating the simple pleasures of life - the warmth of the sun, the scent of rain-soaked earth, the melody of birdsong. It is about realizing that even in our darkest moments, there is always something to be thankful for.

Lastly, nurturing inner peace requires us to be kind to ourselves. Often, we are our own harshest critics, beating ourselves up over perceived failures and flaws. However, it is essential to treat ourselves with the same compassion and understanding we extend to others. It is about recognizing that we are works in progress, that we are learning and growing each day. It is about celebrating our victories, no matter how small, and picking ourselves up when we stumble.

In conclusion, nurturing inner peace is a continuous dance with life. It is about realizing that we are deserving of love, respect, and happiness. It is about living authentically, courageously, joyously. It is about embracing the beautiful, messy, extraordinary adventure that is life, knowing that within us lies an oasis of peace, waiting to be discovered.

## Connecting With the Universe

As we journey through the chapters of self-discovery, self-love, and self-acceptance, we find ourselves standing at the crossroads of our inner world and the vast expanse of the universe. This intersection is where we start to perceive our connection with the cosmos. Our existence is not isolated, we are an integral part of this grand cosmic dance.

The universe isn't an abstract entity existing outside of us. Rather, it is intricately woven into the fabric of our being. Our bodies are made up of the same elements that constitute the universe - carbon, nitrogen, oxygen, and other trace elements. The very atoms that make up our bodies were once part of stars that exploded as supernovae, scattering these elements across the galaxy. In essence, we are stardust, a testament to the universe's incredible creativity.

This connection isn't merely physical. Our thoughts, emotions, and experiences resonate with the energies of the universe, creating a dynamic exchange. Our thoughts and intentions can influence our reality, a concept echoed in the law of attraction. By aligning our energies with the universe, we can manifest our desires into reality. This isn't about bending the universe to our will, but about aligning ourselves with the flow of universal energy.

It's easy to feel small and insignificant in the face of the universe's immensity. However, we need to remember that the universe isn't merely 'out there'; it's also 'in here', within us. We are not separate from the universe; we are the universe experiencing itself.

Understanding this connection fosters a sense of belonging, a realization that we are not alone or isolated. It instills a sense of responsibility towards the universe and all its inhabitants. We start to see the interconnectedness of all things, leading us to live more consciously and compassionately.

Meditation is a powerful tool to strengthen this connection. As we quiet our minds and tune in to our inner selves, we can sense the universe's pulse, its rhythm, its flow. We become more receptive to its wisdom and guidance. We can also connect with the universe through nature, art, music, and other forms of creative expression. These activities help us transcend our limited self and experience our universal self.

Connecting with the universe also invokes a sense of awe and wonder, a reverence for the mystery and majesty of existence. It helps us appreciate the miracle of life, the beauty of creation, and the joy of being. It gives us perspective, reminding us of our place in the cosmic scheme of things. It empowers us to live with purpose, passion, and positivity.

The universe is a mirror reflecting our inner state. If we feel disconnected, it's not because the universe has turned away from us, but because we have turned away from ourselves. By embracing our true selves, we can rekindle our connection with the universe.

In conclusion, connecting with the universe is about realizing our oneness with all of existence. It's about recognizing that we are enough, just as we are. We don't need to be more or do more to validate our existence. We are valuable, we are worthy, and we are loved, simply because we are part of this magnificent universe.

## Finding Meaning and Purpose

Pondering life's purpose and the quest for meaning is a timeless human endeavor. The journey of self-discovery is as unique as each of us, yet we all share the same longing to understand our place in the universe and the significance of our existence. This chapter explores this profound journey and offers insights to help you find your unique purpose, reminding you that you are enough.

Many of us spend our lives seeking external validation, forever chasing the elusive sense of fulfillment that comes from achieving societal standards of success. However, true meaning and purpose are not found in the external world but within ourselves. We are not defined by our accomplishments or possessions, but by our character, values, and the love we share with others.

To find our purpose, we must first understand that our worth is inherent and unchanging. We do not need to prove ourselves to anyone, nor do we need to be more or different than we are now. This realization is liberating. It frees us from the pressures of societal expectations and allows us to focus on our authentic selves.

Purpose often emerges when we align our actions with our deepest values. What matters most to you? What resonates with your spirit? By answering these questions honestly, we can identify our passions and use them as a compass guiding us towards our purpose. We all have unique gifts and talents which, when shared with the world, can create a ripple effect of positivity and change.

However, finding our purpose is a continuous process of self-discovery, growth, and evolution. Our purpose may change over time as we evolve and gain new experiences and insights. It's okay not to have all the answers right now. The important thing is to stay open, curious, and committed to your personal growth.

Furthermore, finding meaning and purpose is not a solitary journey. We are interconnected beings, and our lives are intertwined with those around us. Our actions impact others, just as their actions impact us. Our purpose, therefore, is not just about self-fulfillment but also about contributing to the greater good.

In conclusion, finding meaning and purpose requires honesty, courage, and a willingness to challenge societal norms and expectations. It's about accepting and loving ourselves just as we are, recognizing our inherent worth, and using our unique gifts to make a positive impact in the world. Remember, you are enough, and your life has immense purpose and meaning. Embrace your journey, trust your intuition, and let your heart guide you towards your unique purpose.

# Chapter 15: Manifesting Your Destiny

This is the last chapter of our book and the shortest one. You must be wondering that why this chapter is so short as it is all about what we aspire for in our life. The reason is that if we inculcate all the chapters in our life, most of the things would be there for you as you are perfectly aligned with the true state of nature. When a person is having high values and emotions, they are loved by universe and the Universe gives everything with open hands. The feelings of love, care, compassion, honesty, empathy, and selflessness can bring abundant blessings, acting as a form of magic. By simply envisioning your future and having the correct intentions and trust in the journey, you can attract positivity into your life.

This concept is highlighted in the sacred text, the Bhagavad Gita "You can never get ways with your Karma or actions. Karma is your duty. You have the right to perform your actions, but you are not entitled to the fruits of your actions. Do not let the fruit be the purpose of your actions, and thus you won't be attached to not doing your duty. They start giving magical results as they are very close to Krishna's heart, here we can say God. This approach enables to transcend the limitations of worldly desires and achieve fulfillment."

## Setting Life Goals

Imagine your life as a ship sailing in the vast ocean. Your goals are the compass guiding you towards your destination. Without them, you may find yourself adrift in the sea of life, susceptible to the changing winds and currents. But with a clear destination in mind, the journey becomes more focused, purposeful, and fulfilling.

Setting life goals isn't about creating a rigid roadmap that you must adhere to. It's about aligning your actions with your core values and aspirations. It's about creating a vision for your future that resonates with who you are and what you want from life. I should also resonate with the unique purpose of your life as everyone one his Earth is sent with a special purpose.

In setting these goals, it's important to remember that they are not about proving your worth to others. Your worth is inherent, not contingent on your achievements. Your goals should be about growth, fulfillment, and creating a life that feels meaningful to you. They should be a reflection of your passions, values, and dreams.

You may find that some of your goals are influenced by societal expectations or external pressures. This realization can be challenging, but it's also liberating. It allows you to let go of the goals that don't serve you and focus on those that truly resonate with you.

Your aspirations are like loyal friends accompanying you on the path of self-exploration and self-acceptance. They lead you, push you, and motivate you. They assist you in shaping a life that reflects your true self and your core beliefs. Therefore, embrace this journey with an open heart and an open mind. Define your goals, trust your instincts, and build a life that resonates with purpose.

## Believing In Your Potential

It often requires a level of self-belief that can be challenging to maintain in the face of adversity. However, it is crucial to remember that every individual, including you, is innately capable of achieving greatness.

The first step in believing in your potential is acknowledging your inherent worth. This is easier said than done, especially in a world that frequently measures worth based on external accomplishments. However, it is essential to understand that your value is not determined by your achievements, your status, or the opinions of others. Your worth is inherent, not earned. Once you embrace this truth, you open the door to believing in your potential.

Understanding that you are enough is like planting a seed in fertile soil. Once planted, it needs to be nurtured and cared for to grow. Similarly, believing in your potential requires consistent nurturing. This nurturing comes in the form of positive self-talk, affirmations, and actions that align with your potential. It also requires a certain level of self-awareness to identify and overcome limiting beliefs that might hinder your growth.

Believing in your potential also involves taking risks. Stepping outside of your comfort zone is scary, but it is often where growth happens. It is about pushing boundaries, challenging norms, and daring to dream big. It is about recognizing that failure is not a reflection of your worth but a stepping stone towards success.

It is important to note that believing in your potential does not mean you will not encounter obstacles or setbacks. On the contrary, challenges are part of the journey. They test your resolve, build resilience, and provide valuable lessons that contribute to your growth. Believing in your potential also means being patient with yourself. Growth does not happen overnight. It is a process that requires time, patience, and perseverance. It is about celebrating small victories, learning from setbacks, and continuously striving to be the best version of yourself.

## Taking Inspired Action

Inspired action is not just about doing things but about a unique way of doing them. It's about doing things that are in sync with our heart's desires, our innermost convictions, and our deepest truths. It's about doing things that make us come alive, that make our eyes sparkle, and our hearts flutter with excitement. It's about doing things that make us feel like we are enough, just the way we are.

When we take inspired action, we are not merely reacting to the external circumstances but responding to our inner calling. We are not just following the crowd but forging our own path. We are not just surviving but thriving. We are not just existing but truly living. And in this process, we are not only affirming our inherent worth but also expressing it in the most authentic and empowering way.

Taking inspired action is not always easy. It requires us to confront our fears, overcome our insecurities, and break free from our self-imposed limitations. It requires us to trust ourselves, believe in our dreams, and have faith in our capabilities. It requires us to be vulnerable, to be open, and to be real. But despite these challenges, taking inspired action is the most rewarding and fulfilling experience.

Taking inspired action is like planting a seed. Initially, it may seem like nothing is happening. But with time, patience, and nurture, the seed begins to sprout, grow, and eventually bloom into a beautiful flower. Similarly, when we take inspired action, we may not see immediate results. But with consistency, dedication, and passion, our actions begin to create ripples, bring about changes, and eventually lead to profound transformations. Just remember to keep a positive mindset and an earnest desire to succeed.

Taking inspired action is not about achieving perfection but about embracing progress. It's not about comparing ourselves with others but about celebrating our unique journey. It's not about meeting societal expectations but about fulfilling our personal aspirations. It's not about proving ourselves to the world but about expressing ourselves to the fullest.

When we take inspired action, we are not only empowering ourselves but also inspiring others. We are setting an example, leaving a legacy, and making a difference. We are not only creating a life that we love but also contributing to a world that we envision.

## Creating Your Legacy

As you travel through the journey of life, you will undoubtedly leave traces of your presence along the way. These traces of your existence, your actions, and your impact on the world, will form your legacy. It is something that will outlive you, continuing to influence and inspire long after you're gone. And so, it is crucial to be mindful of the legacy you are creating, because, in the grand tapestry of life, you are enough to make a significant difference.

Consider the term "legacy." It is often associated with grand achievements, with the names of individuals who have left an indelible mark on history. This can be daunting, but it's important to remember that a legacy isn't necessarily about fame or reaching a level of success that is recognized globally. Rather, your legacy is the sum total of your actions, your deeds, and the positive influence you exert in your own sphere of existence. It is about the lives you touch and the positive changes you inspire, no matter how big or small.

In essence, your legacy is the lasting imprint of your unique self on the world. And you are enough to create a legacy that resonates with your values, your passions, and your vision for a better world. You don't have to be a world leader or a billionaire to have a meaningful legacy.

You just need to be you, living your truth and making your unique contribution to the world.

The first step in creating your legacy is to live authentically. Embrace your uniqueness, your strengths, your flaws, your passions, and your dreams. Authenticity is the cornerstone of a meaningful legacy. It's about being true to who you are and using your unique gifts to make a positive impact. It's about being brave enough to show up as your true self, even when it's easier to blend in with the crowd.

Next, consider the values you want your legacy to reflect. Is it kindness, courage, resilience, integrity, or perhaps a combination of these? Your values are the guiding principles of your life, and they should be at the heart of your legacy. It's about living your values every day, making decisions based on them, and weaving them into the fabric of your life.

Your relationships will also shape your legacy. The way you treat others, the love you share, the kindness you spread, these are all part of your legacy. It's about building strong, meaningful relationships based on respect, understanding, and mutual support.

Finally, remember that your legacy is not set in stone. It evolves with you, reflecting your growth and your journey. It's about making a conscious effort to live in a way that aligns with your values, your dreams, and your authentic self. It's about making a positive impact in your own unique way.

Let's start by acknowledging that manifestation is a topic that can spark endless discussions. However, before delving into that, it's important for us to focus on becoming fully alive as human beings. It may sound a bit ironic, but many of us tend to live our lives mechanically, without truly experiencing the richness of life. We go through the motions, only to one day pass away without any meaningful memories. Instead, let's embrace the journey of life and all that it has to offer. By doing so, we will find that the universe is always ready to provide us with what is truly best for our lives, rather than simply fulfilling our desires. Believe in this truth and approach life with a deep sense of gratitude, and you will find that everything you want will come to you.

We've reached the conclusion of this wonderful adventure through the pages of "Stick to Basics". Feel free to revisit any chapter whenever you need guidance, inspiration, or a shoulder to lean on. Always remember, you are enough.

# About Author

Yatika Tyagi, is no one but your friend who is trying to introduce you with yourself. Professionally she is running a business. She inspired by emotional well being and human nature, Yatika penned down a book where she connecting people with themselves. It's her endeavor to make you enough- just the way you are. She is making you realize that you are happy with your imperfections in this perfect world. She not only enlightens readers but also inspires them to deepen their connection with themselves. Through her descriptive approach, Yatika writing resonates with authenticity and emotion, leaving a lasting impact on anyone who is reading this book. With her writing she is inspiring reader to live a life full of love, happiness, compassion and wholeness.

Since her schooling days, she took interest in literature, creative works like- writing and collecting quotations and gradually enjoying pen down her feelings in the form of poetic verses in the pages of her diary.

www.ingramcontent.com/pod-product-compliance
Lightning Source LLC
LaVergne TN
LVHW012054160826
845678LV00014B/2815

* 9 7 8 8 1 9 7 1 0 2 3 5 6 *